D1452146

BR Motive Power Since 1948

72009

BR Motive Power Since 1948

B.K.COOPER

IA
LONDON
IAN ALLAN LTD

First published 1985

ISBN 0 7110 1496 5

Published by Ian Allan Ltd, Shepperton, Surrey; and printed by Ian Allan Printing Ltd at their works at Coombelands in Runnymede, England.

Half Title
With the spans of the Forth Bridge in the background, an English Electric Type 4, later Class 40, at the head of the Aberdeen-Edinburgh train passes 'Britannia' Pacific No 70003 *John Bunyan* on a Perth-Millerhill van train at Dalmeny Junction in December 1965. *W. J. V. Anderson*

Title
BR Standard 'Clan' class Pacific No 72009 *Clan Stewart* climbs towards Beattock summit with the 9.25 am Crewe-Perth and Aberdeen on 11 August 1964. *J. S. Whiteley*

Below:
Newly built 2,200hp 'Warship' class No D810 *Cockade* leaves Bristol Temple Meads with the down 'Devonian' on 28 September 1959. *M. Mensing*

Contents

Front cover, top:
Class 7 'Britannia' Pacific No 70020 *Mercury* seen at Swindon in October 1956.
T. G. Flinders

Front cover, centre:
Class 87 No 87.001 *Royal Scot* threads the Lune Valley with the 13.23 Edinburgh-Taunton train on 22 March 1980. *P. J. Robinson*

Front cover, bottom:
Side view of Class 50 locomotive.

Abbreviations

AEI	Associated Electrical Industries Ltd
AWS	Automatic Warning System
BFB	Bulleid-Firth-Brown
BRB	British Railways Board
BRCW	Birmingham Railway Carriage & Wagon Co Ltd
BREL	British Railways Engineering Ltd
BTH	British Thomson Houston Co Ltd
CME	Chief Mechanical Engineer
DMU	Diesel Multiple Unit
ECML	East Coast main line
EE	English Electric Co Ltd
EMU	Electric Multiple Unit
ER	Eastern Region (BR)
ETH	Electric Train Heating
GEC	General Electric Co Ltd
LMR	London Midland Region (BR)
MAN	Maschinenfabrik Augsburg Nürnberg AG
MGR	Merry-go-round
NBL	North British Locomotive Co Ltd
SAB	SAB Nife AB
ScR	Scottish Region (BR)
SLM	Schweizerische Lokomotiv-und Maschinenfabrik
SR	Southern Region (BR)
WCML	West Coast main line
WR	Western Region (BR)

Brand new 'AL1' class, later Class 81, 25kV ac electric locomotive No E3001, the first of a new generation of BR motive power, which appeared in December 1959. *Metropolitan-Vickers*

Preface

Historians of locomotive design after 1948 may consider the period lacking in big names and personalities. Electric and diesel-electric locomotives are the products of design teams whose members often remain anonymous and are unlikely to acquire the status of Old Testament prophets gained by some of their predecessors in the steam age. This is unfair considering the complexity of the problems they faced and the decisions they had to take in organising the change from steam to diesel and electric traction on British Railways. It is hard not to feel that some of the old masters who now inhabit the steam locomotive engineer's pantheon got there by a bit of luck and something equivalent to the gardener's 'green fingers' in hitting upon the combination of heating surface, boiler pressure and valve characteristics that produced a classic locomotive.

The landmarks of the post-nationalisation period have been the locomotives themselves rather than the personalities behind them. Some designs faltered, or tried to do too much too soon, but the ideas were often right, and have been proved right as better means have been found for putting them into practice. This survey charts progress from the standard steam classes to the latest diesel-electric workhorse. There have been tentative experiments with gas turbines, and a more successful application of diesel-hydraulic power. In electric traction Britain has shed its image of a dc country and gone whole-heartedly for the 25kV ac system, and in that connection the name of S. B. Warder will certainly be remembered by posterity for the energy and conviction with which he moved British Railways and the British electrical industry towards accepting the change. For years British practice has remained faithful to the Bo-Bo locomotive so strongly recommended by the 'founding fathers' of 50Hz traction in France but the emergence of a Co-Co design reflects the course of events across the Channel some years ago when a *volte face* in favour of six motored axles was executed with Gallic finesse, although not pursued for long.

In diesel traction the dominant trend has been the increase in power per cylinder, coupled with the brushless alternator that has made the power available at the rails without the commutation problems of the large traction generator delivering a high output at a relatively high rotational speed. Among enthusiasts attitudes to diesels have changed remarkably. At first they were viewed with hostility. Today some of those which have left the scene are remembered with affection. They have had the advantage over the electric locomotive of appealing to the ear as well as to the eye and there are many who listen with rapt attention to recordings of the Deltic roar, the Sulzer bark and so on, and who risk their necks on railtours by leaning out of carriage windows the better to hear these stirring drumbeats.

In putting on record the distinctive features of all locomotives since 1948, some omissions have been necessary on grounds of space.

In particular it would not be feasible to give such detailed coverage of the numerous small diesel shunter designs. Several borderline cases would have slipped through the net but for the vigilance of Andrew Fox of Ian Allan Ltd, whose assistance was also invaluable in the selection and captioning of photographs and presentation of data. But all locomotives – the good, the bad and the indifferent – acquire the qualities praised by Hilaire Belloc in certain university dons. They remain as landmarks on the horizon of our memories 'like large and comfortable trees'.

B. K. Cooper

1 Non-Standard Steam Locomotives

With the nationalisation of Britain's railways in 1948, the construction of various pre-nationalisation classes was continued until such time as a new standard series of steam locomotives could be designed for British Railways. This book does not cover the various classes which had been introduced before nationalisation, of which further examples were built for the new administration. Only those designs are dealt with which first appeared after nationalisation and therefore never carried the liveries of the 'Big Four' companies from which their designs originated. The Bulleid Pacifics are included since their rebuilding was so major as to create an essentially new class of locomotive.

'1500' Class 0-6-0PT

Number series: 1500-1509
Cylinders: Two, 17.5in × 24in
Heating surface:
Tubes: 1,245.7sq ft
Firebox: 101.7sq ft
Total: 1,347.4sq ft
Grate area: 17.4sq ft
Boiler pressure: 200lb/sq in
Wheel arrangement: 0-6-0PT
Valve gear: Walschaerts
Driving wheel dia: 4ft 7.5in
TE at 85% pressure: 22,515lb
Weight: 58ton 3cwt
First loco built: June 1949
Last loco withdrawn: December 1963

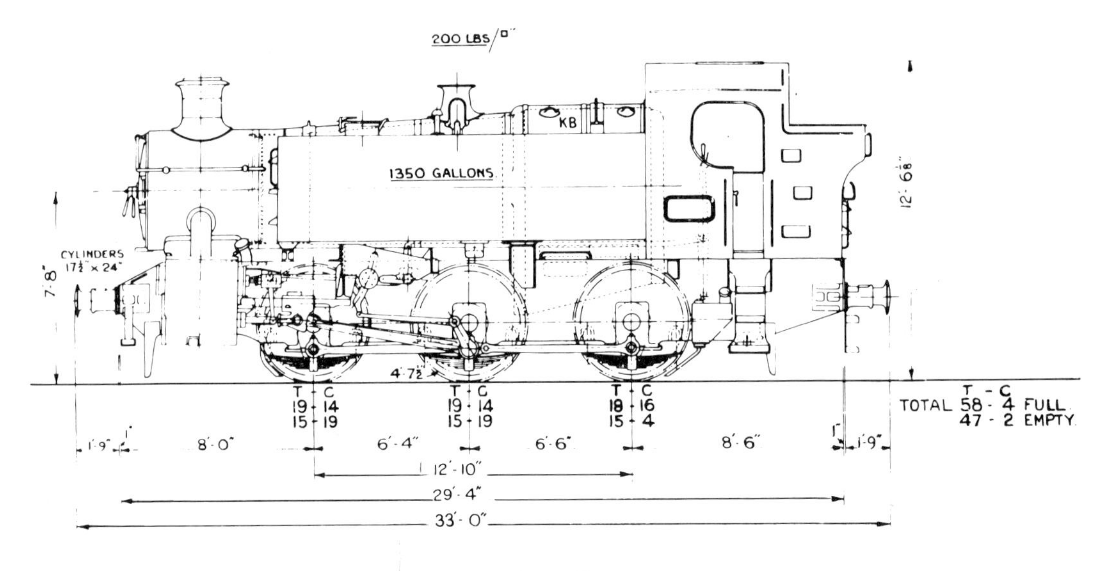

Above:
General arrangement of outside cylinder '1500' class 0-6-0PT of 1949.

The first new design of locomotive to appear on the Western Region after nationalisation was an outside-cylinder 0-6-0 shunting tank, introduced in 1949. There was a departure from previous

Swindon practice in the use of outside Walschaerts valve gear for the two cyclinders. This layout made almost all the running gear accessible from ground level so that the engine could be prepared and all periodical examinations carried out without recourse to a pit. To some extent the locomotive offered certain advantages of the diesel shunter in being able to perform long periods of shunting without returning to a shed. The side tanks carried 1,350gal of water and the bunker capacity was 3ton 3cwt of coal.

Left:
The distinctive appearance of the '1500' class 0-6-0PT is visible in this view of No 1504 inside Old Oak Common roundhouse in August 1958. Note the outside Walschaerts valve gear and lack of a running plate. *B. Morrison*

'1600' Class 0-6-0PT

Number series: 1600-1669
Cylinders: Two, 16.5in × 24in
Heating surface:
  Tubes: 877.2sq ft
  Firebox: 79.5sq ft
  Total: 956.7sq ft
Grate area: 14.9sq ft
Boiler pressure: 165lb/sq in

Wheel arrangement: 0-6-0PT
Valve gear: Stephenson
Driving wheel dia: 4ft 1.5in
TE at 85% pressure: 18,515lb
Weight: 41ton 12cwt
First loco built: October 1949
Last loco withdrawn: August 1966

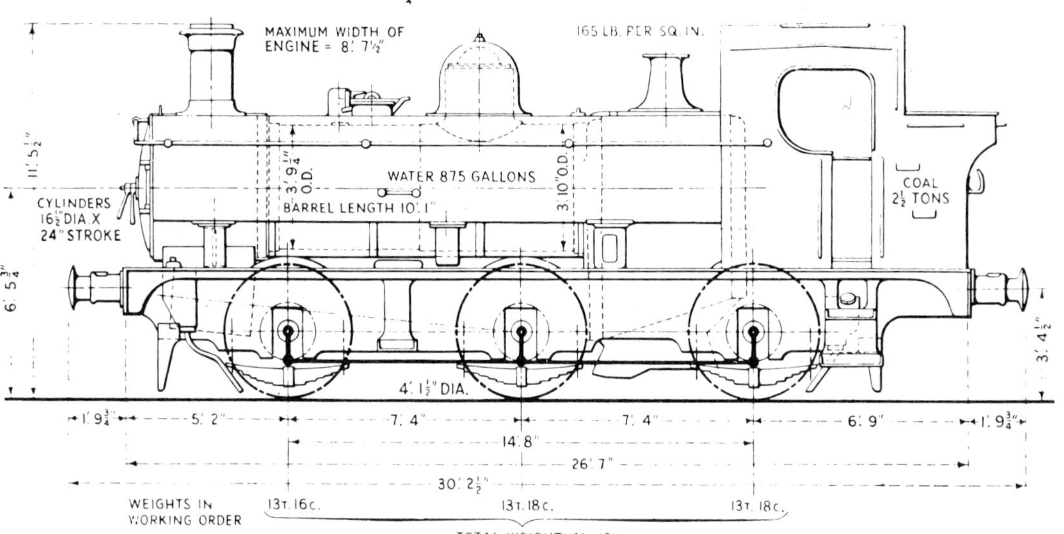

Below:
General arrangement of Western Region '1600' class 0-6-0PT of 1949.

In late 1949 there appeared from Swindon Works the final Great Western Railway design to be built. This was the '1600' class of pannier tanks, of which construction somewhat surprisingly continued until 1955. In contrast with the strikingly new '1500' class, the '1600' represented a return to the traditional inside cylinder GWR pannier tank design, their appearance and construction being of a

very familiar pattern. Indeed the '1600' class was in many respects almost identical to the aged '2021' class which it was built to replace.

The last batch was of note in being the final examples of the six-coupled shunting tank to be built for British Railways.

Above:
In contrast to the '1500's, the '1600' class of pannier tank, also introduced in 1949, presented a thoroughly traditional appearance, as exemplified by No 1647. *P. J. Sharpe*

Peppercorn 'A1' Pacific

Number series: 60114-60162
Cylinders: Three, 19in × 26in
Heating surface:
Tubes: 2,216.1sq ft
Firebox: 245.3sq ft
Superheater: 679.6sq ft
Total: 3,141sq ft
Grate area: 50sq ft
Boiler pressure: 250lb/sq in

Wheel arrangement: 4-6-2
Valve gear: Walschaerts
Driving wheel dia: 6ft 8in
TE at 85% pressure: 37,397lb
Weight: Loco: 104ton 2cwt
Tender: 60ton 7cwt
First loco built: August 1948
Last loco withdrawn: June 1966

Below:
General arrangement of Peppercorn 'A1' class 4-6-2 of 1948.

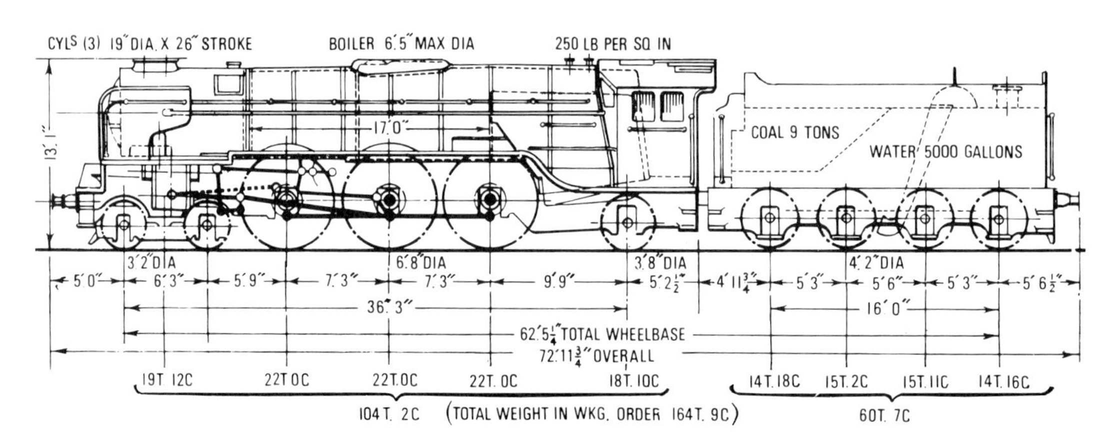

Above:
Peppercorn 'A1' Pacific No 60153 *Flamboyant* is seen leaving York on a down express in April 1956.
P. Ransome-Wallis

In 1945 the CME of the London and North Eastern Railway, Edward Thompson, was responsible for the highly controversial rebuilding of the original Gresley Pacific, No 4470 *Great Northern*, as the prototype for a new mixed traffic Pacific design. The 'rebuild' was in fact so drastic as to leave very little of the original locomotive. This engine eventually became the sole example of Class A1/1.

Although authority was given in the same year for the construction of a new series of 'A1' class Pacific locomotives, little was done for some time. When the new locomotives were actually proceeded with, Thompson had retired and been succeeded by A. H. Peppercorn. As a result, considerable changes were made in the production build relative to the prototype 'A1/1'. The new 'A1' class locomotives had their cylinders located in the normal position in line with the bogie (on the 'A1/1' they had been behind the rear bogie wheels) and carried the same boiler as the Peppercorn 'A2' but fitted with Kylchap double chimney.

Being delivered shortly after nationalisation, the 'A1' class did not carry LNER numbers or initials, instead appearing at first in LNER green with 'British Railways' on the tender.

Nos 60153-60157 were fitted with Timken roller bearings on all axles, resulting in considerably increased mileages run between repairs.

Peppercorn 'K1' 2-6-0

Number series: 62001-62070
Cylinders: Two, 20in × 26in
Heating surface:
Tubes: 1,240sq ft
Firebox: 168sq ft
Superheater: 300sq ft
Total: 1,708sq ft
Grate area: 27.9sq ft
Boiler pressure: 225lb/sq in
Wheel arrangement: 2-6-0
Valve gear: Walschaerts
Driving wheel dia: 5ft 2in
TE at 85% pressure: 32,081lb
Weight: Loco: 66ton 0cwt
Tender: 52ton 0cwt
First loco built: May 1949
Last loco withdrawn: December 1967

In 1945 three-cylinder Gresley 'K4' No 3445 *MacCailin Mor* was rebuilt by Thompson as a two-cylinder locomotive fitted with a shortened version of the 'B1' class boiler. No further 'K4' conversions were authorised however. Instead a new build of locomotives to the pattern of the rebuild was ordered from the North British Locomotive Company by A. H. Peppercorn, who had taken over from Thompson as CME. Although ordered by the LNER, these locomotives did not

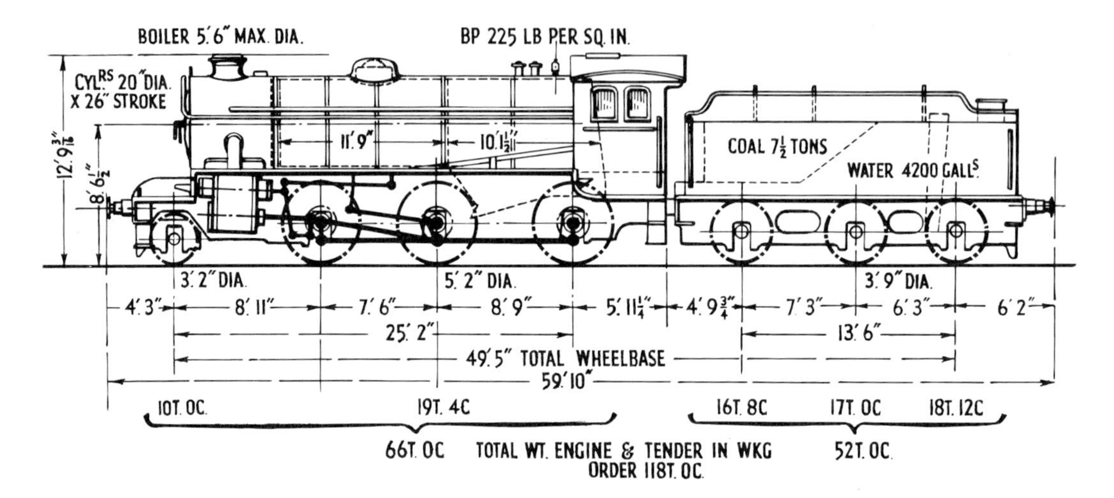

Above:
General arrangement of Peppercorn 'K1' class 2-6-0 of 1948.

actually appear until British Railways days and therefore never carried LNER livery.

The prototype was classified 'K1/1' whilst the new locomotives became Class K1. They differed in several details from the prototype, featuring modified frames and having larger 4,200gal tenders.

Below:
The other LNER design introduced in British Railways days was the 'K1' 2-6-0, of which 70 examples were built. No 62060 is seen at York shed on 4 October 1964.
B. Stephenson

Rebuilt Bulleid Pacifics

Number series: 35001-35030*
Cylinders: Three, 18in × 24in
Heating surface:
Tubes: 2,176sq ft
Firebox: 275sq ft
Superheater: 612sq ft
Total: 3,063sq ft
Grate area: 48.5sq ft
Boiler pressure: 250lb/sq in

Wheel arrangement: 4-6-2
Valve gear: Walschaerts
Driving wheel dia: 6ft 2in
TE at 85% pressure: 33,495lb
Weight: Loco: 97ton 18cwt
Tender: 47ton 16cwt*
First loco built: June 1941
First loco rebuilt: February 1956
Last loco withdrawn: July 1967

† Nos 35001-35020 originally numbered 21C1-21C20
* Refers to 5,000 gal tender. Other tender types also used.

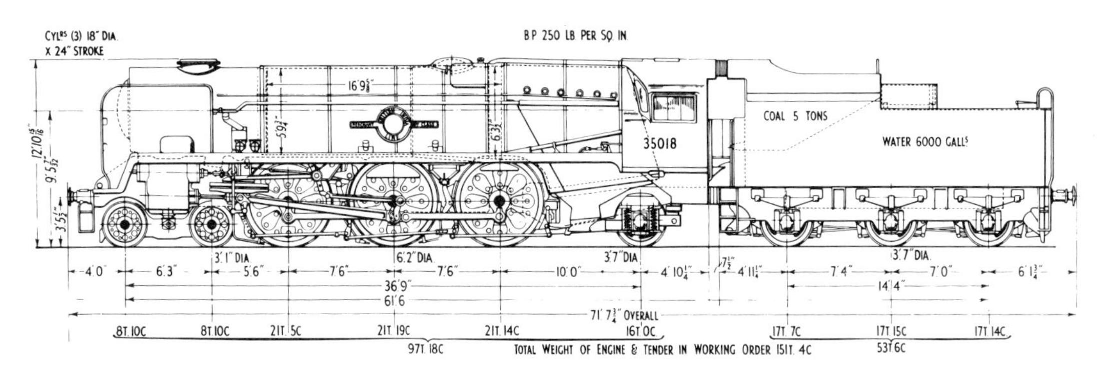

Below:
General arrangement of Bulleid 'Merchant Navy' class 4-6-2 as rebuilt from 1956.

Number series: 34001-34110†
Cylinders: Three, 16.4in × 24in
Heating surface:
Tubes: 1,869sq ft
Firebox: 253sq ft
Superheater: 488sq ft
Total: 2,610sq ft
Grate area: 38.25sq ft
Boiler pressure: 250lb/sq in

† Nos 34001-34070 originally numbered 21C101-21C170

Wheel arrangement: 4-6-2
Valve gear: Walschaerts
Driving wheel dia: 6ft 2in
TE at 85% pressure: 27,715lb
Weight: Loco: 90ton 1cwt
Tender: 42ton 12cwt*
First loco built: June 1945
First loco rebuilt: June 1957
Last loco withdrawn: July 1967

* Refers to 4,500gal tender. Other tender types also used.

O. V. S. Bulleid's design of Pacific locomotives for the Southern Railway did not meet the easy maintenance and high availability criteria set by British Railways for its steam fleet. Rebuilding of the 'Merchant Navy' class began in 1956. The 'air-smoothed' boiler casing was removed but the boiler was unchanged. Working pressure had been reduced already from 280 to 250lb/sq in. The outside cylinders were retained but a new inside cylinder with a repositioned piston valve was provided. Three sets of Walschaerts valve gear replaced the original gear with its chain drive and oil bath, which had been troublesome to adjust and prone to leakage of oil. Manual reverse gear replaced the steam reverser, with which it had been difficult to set the cut-off accurately. The smokebox, with large diameter chimney, and the saddle were new. Running plates similar to those of the 'Britannia' class were fitted. The box type coupled wheels were the most recognisable survivals of the engines as built. Known as BFB wheels, they were a variant devised by Bulleid and

Top:
Although the appearance of Bulleid's 'Merchant Navy' Pacifics was transformed when they were rebuilt from 1956 onwards, the characteristic Boxpok wheels remained as clearly seen in this view of No 35023 *Holland-Afrika Line*. *G. H. Marsh*

Above:
Many of the lightweight Pacifics of the 'West Country'/'Battle of Britain' class were rebuilt similarly to the 'Merchant Navy' class. No 34098 *Templecombe* is seen leaving Southampton Central for Bournemouth on 6 March 1961. *J. C. Haydon*

the firm of Thos Firth & John Brown of the Boxpok wheel. All the 'Merchant Navies' were eventually rebuilt in this way.

In June 1945 the first of a series of lighter Pacifics, similar to the 'Merchant Navies' in their original form, had been placed in service by the Southern Railway. These 110 locomotives formed the 'West Country' class although later ones in the series had names associated with the Battle of Britain. From No 34001 to 34070 they were 8ft 6in wide over the cabs so as to be able to work on the Tonbridge-Hastings section but the requirement to do so did not arise and from 34071 onwards the width was 9ft. Rebuilding on lines similar to those followed in the 'Merchant Navies' was undertaken by BR, the first rebuild appearing in June 1957. The work did not extend to the whole class for the rebuilds were heavier than the originals and prohibited from certain routes on which the latter were permitted. Only the Plymouth road was open to them west of Exeter. The cabs in all rebuilds were widened to 9ft.

2 The Standard Steam Classes

In 1948 British Railways was only beginning to gain practical experience of main line diesel working. Main line electric traction was confined to the Southern Region and was predominantly an EMU operation, only three electric locomotives being in service. There could be no thought of a quick transition to one of the alternatives to the steam locomotive but it would not have been economic to maintain the 448 different types then in service because of the diversity of spares required. It was therefore decided to reduce the locomotive fleet to 10 standard classes, which would be designed to meet the following objectives (see paper read by E. S. Cox to the Institution of Locomotive Engineers on 21 March 1951):

1 Utmost in steam-producing capacity permitted by weight and dimensions.
2 Simplicity, with least number of working parts, all readily visible and accessible.
3 Each type to be proportioned to give the widest range of mixed traffic working.
4 High level of bearing performance by using roller bearings throughout for road wheels where financially justified.
5 Simplified shed preparation by extended use of mechanical lubricators and grease lubrication.
6 Reduction in work of disposal by means of self-cleaning smokebox, rocking grate and self-emptying ashpan.
7 Engines to be made as sure-footed as possible by high factors of adhesion, sensitive regulator and efficient sanding gear.
8 Within the above requirements, thermal efficiency to be sought by larger grate areas, promoting low rates of combustion under average working conditions, but high degree superheat and by long lap valve gear.

Thermal, operating and maintenance efficiency were recognised as difficult to achieve in combination, as high standards in any two usually meant a falling off in the third. It was therefore decided to concentrate on higher availability and lower maintenance costs rather than to seek markedly higher thermal efficiency, as the first two brought a more certain reward. All designs were to be two-cylinder engines because:

1 Only thus could the ultimate in simplicity and accessibility be reached.
2 The split inside big end was a source of trouble at high speeds and powers unless exceptional integrity of maintenance could be achieved.
3 A crank axle is expensive in first cost and maintenance.
4 Theoretically multi-cylinder engines should be better at starting but this was not observable in practice.
5 Four exhausts per revolution in general promote better steaming than do six or eight, other things being equal.

Eventually 11 classes of standard two-cylinder engines were built. There was also one prototype three-cylinder Pacific, No 71000 *Duke of Gloucester*, but this was overtaken by the modernisation plan with its switch to diesel and electric traction and there was no follow-up.

Four of the first six standard designs to be announced were adaptations of former types to conform with BR principles, but the two Pacifics, Class 7 and Class 6, were completely new, although embodying the best features of the previous railway companies' express passenger designs. Drawing office work for the standard classes was shared between Brighton, Derby, Doncaster and Swindon, each being responsible for certain components. For each class one works was nominated as 'parent' and produced the general arrangement drawings, although the 'parent' works did not necessarily build the class or classes for which it was responsible. Principal characteristics of the various 'BR Standards' are summarised in the following paragraphs.

Class 7 'Britannia' Pacifics

Number series: 70000-70054
Cylinders: Two, 20in × 28in
Heating surface:
Tubes: 2,264sq ft
Firebox: 210sq ft
Superheater: 704sq ft
Total: 3,178sq ft
Grate area: 42sq ft
Boiler pressure: 250lb/sq in

Wheel arrangement: 4-6-2
Valve gear: Walschaerts
Driving wheel dia: 6ft 2in
TE at 85% pressure: 32,150lb
Weight: Loco: 94ton 4cwt
Tender: 49ton 3cwt*
First loco built: January 1951
Last loco withdrawn: August 1968

* Refers to BR1 tender. Other tender types also used.

Below:
General arrangement of BR Standard 70000 'Britannia' Class 7 4-6-2 designed at Derby, with BR1A tender.

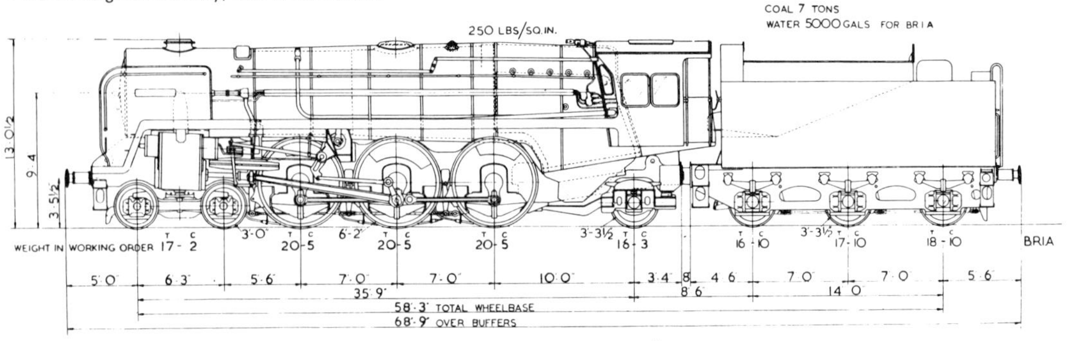

MINIMUM RADIUS CURVE WITHOUT GAUGE WIDENING 6 CHAINS (4½ CHAINS DEAD SLOW)

The first order for 'Britannia' Pacifics was for 25 locomotives. Ultimately there were 55 in the class, all built at Crewe but of Derby 'parentage'. Their first allocation was to Stratford and Norwich sheds for service between Liverpool Street and East Anglia. No 70000 arrived in the Region on 1 February 1951 and by the time a recast timetable was introduced in the summer, 12 engines were available. In the new schedules the London-Norwich time by the principal expresses was reduced from 2hr 20min to 2hr 10min. Troubles soon occurred. A centrifugal steam drier under the dome failed to live up to its name and water tended to be carried over to the cylinders, resulting in broken pistons. A modification having failed to provide a cure, the drier was replaced by a simple pipe steam intake but the point of entry was over 4in higher above the boiler water level than in the original arrangement. A deeper dome cover was fitted.

A deeper-seated problem was foreshadowed by a succession of bent coupling rods. This was not unusual in new locomotives before drivers were accustomed to them, but when a coupling rod broke while No 70004 was hauling the up 'Golden Arrow' Pullman boat train at Headcorn, the whole class was withdrawn for examination. It was found that the stresses which had bent the rods had also shifted the wheels on their axles. The use of roller bearings made it necessary for the wheel seat to be of smaller diameter than the bearing journal. The seat was ground to a taper of 1 in 500 and the keys were shallower than usual. At this point also, the axle was bored out to save weight. It was concluded that when the wheel was pressed on, the hollow axle was only just able to bear the load without deformation. The axle was therefore plugged, the wheel seat ground parallel and the keyways deepened. Boring out an axle to reduce weight was a long-established practice but in the 'Britannias' the axle-loads were within the limits without resorting to it. With the new arrangements the wheel shifting problems did not recur.

The bending and breaking of coupling rods was caused by high lateral stresses when the wheels had shifted. Originally the rods were fluted (I-section) but after this episode, rods of uniform rectangular section were used for the leading pair of coupled wheels. At a later stage the rear pair of coupling rods were replaced by others of similar rectangular section. I-section connecting rods were retained. Some later builds had roller bearings on the driving axles only, or plain bearings on all coupled axles.

With their 6ft 2in coupled wheels fully exposed by the high running plate, the 'Britannias' clearly proclaimed themselves as mixed traffic locomotives, carrying on a tradition of versatility that had begun in the 1930s with 'Black Fives' and 'Green Arrows' and was more necessary than ever in the utilitarian postwar era with the steam locomotive under increasing challenge. But they were still fast engines. The late Cecil J. Allen recorded a run with No 70035 *Rudyard Kipling* on the down 'Broadsman' when the 46.3 miles from Ipswich to Norwich Thorpe were run start to stop in 39min 7 sec with an average speed of 84.4mph for 26½ miles and a maximum of 94mph at Diss.

A uniform cab layout was adopted for the BR Standard locomotives and was seen for the first time in the 'Britannias'. Instruments were grouped for easy observation, those on the side opposite the driver being angled towards him. Two linked pull-out handles, one on each side of the cab, controlled the regulator. The reverser handwheel was edge-on but opinions differed as to whether this made it easier to adjust. Front windows were set at an angle to eliminate reflections. The outlook from the cab was criticised, however, after an accident at Milton, near Didcot, on the Western Region on 20 November 1955 when the driver of No 70026 *Polar Star* failed to see that he was being diverted from the main to the goods line and took the points at 55mph instead of 10mph. The engine was derailed, 11 persons killed and 157 injured. It was concluded that the driver's forward vision had been obstructed by the handrails on the outer face of the smoke deflectors and their removal was recommended. They were replaced by handholds let into the plates. Inside the cab, the firebox face was commendably uncluttered. Piping runs were few and tidily arranged. Steam supplies were taken from a common manifold outside the cab. The footplate floor was extended back on cantilever brackets to meet the front face of the tender, dispensing with the conventional fall plate. In practice the cabs were draughty and this fault was only partly overcome by canvas screens, and later rubber bellows, between engine and tender.

'Britannia' No 70013 *Oliver Cromwell* was the longest survivor of the class, remaining in service until August 1968. In their day the 'Britannias' worked on all Regions of British Railways and maintained the prestige of the British main line steam locomotive to the end. O. S. Nock said of them: 'If this last British example of a powerful locomotive intended for express passenger as well as mixed traffic duties was a hard-slogging work-horse rather than a highly-bred racer, it was an ample sign of the times.' (Nock, O. S. *The British Steam Railway Locomotive. Vol 2, 1925 to 1965.* Ian Allan Ltd, 1966.)

Below:
Class 7 'Britannia' Pacific No 70037 *Hereward the Wake.* This locomotive is fitted with modified smoke deflectors on which clearly visible hand holds have replaced handrails which were considered to interfere with the view from the cab. Note also rectangular section coupling rods, replacing the original fluted version. *P. Ransome-Wallis*

Class 8MT Pacific No 71000

Number series: 71000
Cylinders: Three, 18in × 26in
Heating surface:
Tubes: 2,364sq ft
Firebox: 226sq ft
Superheater: 691sq ft
Total: 3,281sq ft
Grate area: 48.6sq ft
Boiler pressure: 250lb/sq in

Wheel arrangement: 4-6-2
Valve gear: Caprotti
Driving wheel dia: 6ft 2in
TE at 85% pressure: 39,080lb
Weight: Loco: 101ton 5cwt
Tender: 53ton 14cwt
Loco built: June 1954
Loco withdrawn: December 1962

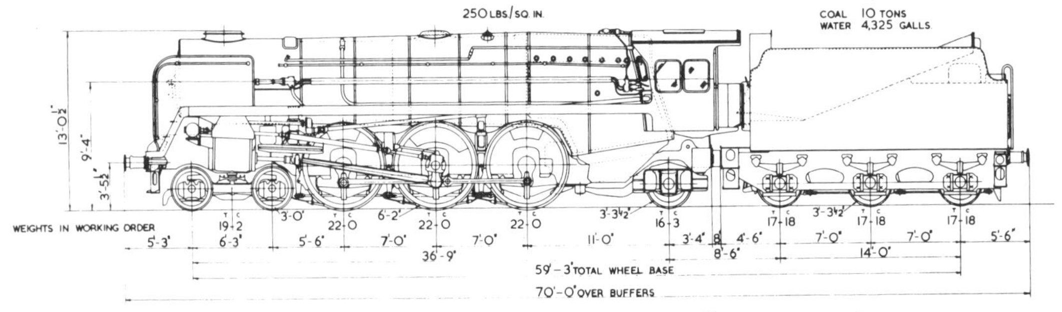

Only one of the BR Standard designs was in the express passenger Class 8P category and it remained unique. This was the Pacific No 71000 *Duke of Gloucester* built at Crewe in April 1954 and put into traffic from Crewe North MPD in June of that year. It was not an auspicious period for steam, being close to the announcement of BR's modernisation plan with its switch to diesel and electric traction, and No 71000 ended its working life with BR in December 1962. The locomotive was built as a replacement for LMR Pacific No 46202 *Princess Anne*, destroyed in the accident at Harrow in October 1952. No 46202 was a rebuild of the LMS 'Turbomotive' as a standard Princess 'Royal Pacific'. The objective in No 71000 was a similar tractive effort (a nominal 40,000lb) and the capacity to sustain high power outputs. In spite of

Above:
General arrangement of BR Standard No 71000 *Duke of Gloucester* Class 8 4-6-2 designed at Derby, with BR1J tender.

Below:
The solitary Standard Class 8 Pacific, No 71000 *Duke of Gloucester* is seen not long after entering service, heading the northbound 'Mid-Day Scot' north of Oxenholme in late evening sunshine on 17 September 1954. *J. D. Mills*

the 'express passenger' category, the same 6ft 2in wheel diameter as in the 'Britannias' was retained, these engines having shown themselves able to run freely at 90 mph. Heating surfaces were also similar to the 'Britannia' class but there was a larger grate area and a double blastpipe and chimney. The other distinctive features of the engine were poppet valve gear and three cylinders. The third cylinder was a departure from the principles laid down for the standard classes but No 71000 could trace its origin back to a proposal in 1948 for a four-cylinder Pacific.

The cylinder efficiency of No 71000 was high and encouraged the use of poppet valves in 30 of the Standard Class 5 4-6-0s at a later date, but boiler performance was disappointing. Further tests were needed to arrive at a correct balance between the boiler and the draughting arrangements. They were never carried out, because the end of the steam era on British Railways was already in sight. Stationed at Crewe North, the engine first worked on the West Coast main line, one of its regular turns being on the 'Mid-Day Scot'. Its characteristics were later explored in detail on the Swindon test plant and in road tests on the Western Region, followed by further work on the West Coast main line. Between Carnforth and Carlisle, the engine once recorded a gain of nearly 7min on the 73min schedule for the 63 miles including Shap Summit, but its coal consumption was heavy and it was not popular with the crews. No 71000 was withdrawn from service on 1 December 1962, its secrets still unsolved.

Class 6 'Clan' Pacifics

Number series: 72000-72009
Cylinders: Two, 19.5in × 28in
Heating surface:
Tubes: 1,878sq ft
Firebox: 195sq ft
Superheater: 615sq ft
Total: 2,688sq ft
Grate area: 36sq ft
Boiler pressure: 225lb/sq in
Wheel arrangement: 4-6-2
Valve gear: Walschaerts
Driving wheel dia: 6ft 2in
TE at 85% pressure: 27,520lb
Weight: Loco: 86ton 19cwt
Tender: 49ton 3cwt
First loco built: December 1951
Last loco withdrawn: April 1966

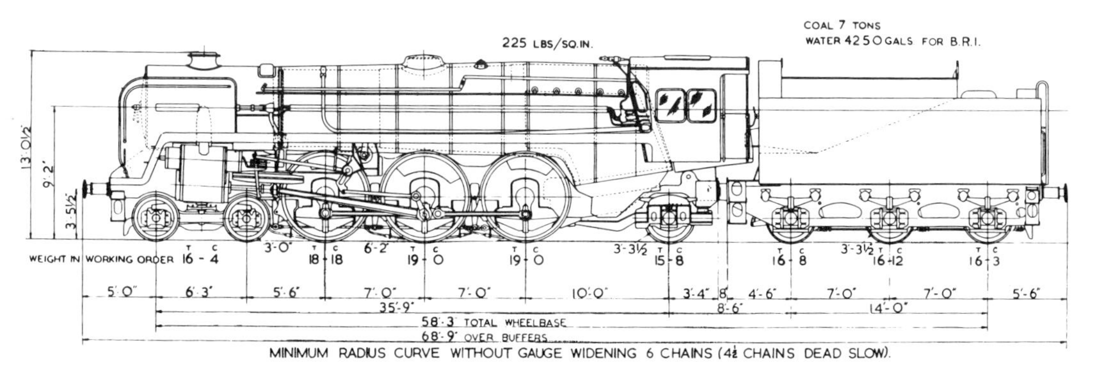

Above:
General arrangement of BR Standard 72000 'Clan' Class 6 4-6-2 designed at Derby, with BR1 tender.

A second Pacific in the BR Standard locomotive range was a 'scaled-down' version of the 'Britannia' classified 6MT. Maximum axle-load was 19ton compared with the 'Britannia's' 20ton 5cwt. It had the same chassis as the 'Britannia' class but a smaller boiler and cylinders. Coupled wheels, roller bearings and bored-out axles were the same as in the 'Britannias' before modification and remained unchanged throughout the life of the class, no wheel-shifting problems being experienced.

These ten light Pacifics were generally known as the 'Clan' class for the naming theme, which was consistent throughout, whereas the 'Britannias' dipped into a variety of sources for inspiration – historical, literary, and finally geographical with six engines named after Scottish firths. Derby was the parent design office and the engines were all built at Crewe. All were allotted to the Scottish Region. After running-in turns between Crewe and Shrewsbury, and a trial in the Birmingham area which included a run to London, they departed to Carlisle (Kingmoor) and Polmadie (Glasgow).

Subsequently their appearances South of the Border were on trains between Glasgow, Manchester and Liverpool. In Scotland they worked Stranraer boat trains from both Glasgow and Carlisle, and other duties took them northwards to Dundee, Perth and Aberdeen.

Above:
Class 6 'Clan' Pacific No 72008 *Clan Macleod* waits at Carlisle to take over a down Scottish express on 8 June 1963. Only 10 locomotives of this class, a small boilered version of the 'Britannia' class were ever built. *I. S. Carr*

Standard 4-6-0s

Number series: 73000-73171
Cylinders: Two, 19in × 28in
Heating surface:
Tubes: 1,479sq ft
Firebox: 171sq ft
Superheater: 369sq ft
Total: 2,019sq ft
Grate area: 28.65sq ft
Boiler pressure: 225lb/sq in

Wheel arrangement: 4-6-0
Valve gear: Walschaerts
Driving wheel dia: 6ft 2in
TE at 85% pressure: 26,120lb
Weight: Loco: 76ton 4cwt
Tender: 49ton 3cwt*
First loco built: April 1951
Last loco withdrawn: May 1968

Note: Nos 73125-73154 fitted with Caprotti valve gear
* Refers to BR1 tender. Other tender types also used. BR1F tender 55ton 5cwt.

Below:
General arrangement of BR Standard 73000 Class 5 4-6-0 designed at Doncaster, as fitted with BR1F tender for Southern Region.

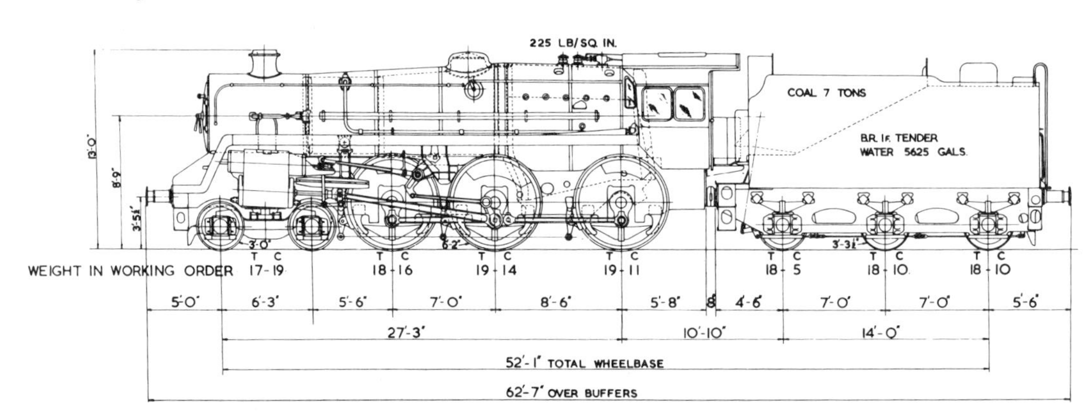

Number series: 75000-75079
Cylinders: Two, 18in × 28in
Heating surface:
Tubes: 1,301sq ft
Firebox: 143sq ft
Superheater: 265sq ft
Total: 1,709sq ft
Grate area: 26.7sq ft
Boiler pressure: 225lb/sq in

Wheel arrangement: 4-6-0
Valve gear: Walschaerts
Driving wheel dia: 5ft 8in
TE at 85% pressure: 25,100lb
Weight: Loco: 69ton 0cwt
Tender: 42ton 3cwt*
First loco built: May 1951
Last loco withdrawn: February 1968

* Refers to BR2 tender. Other tender types also used.

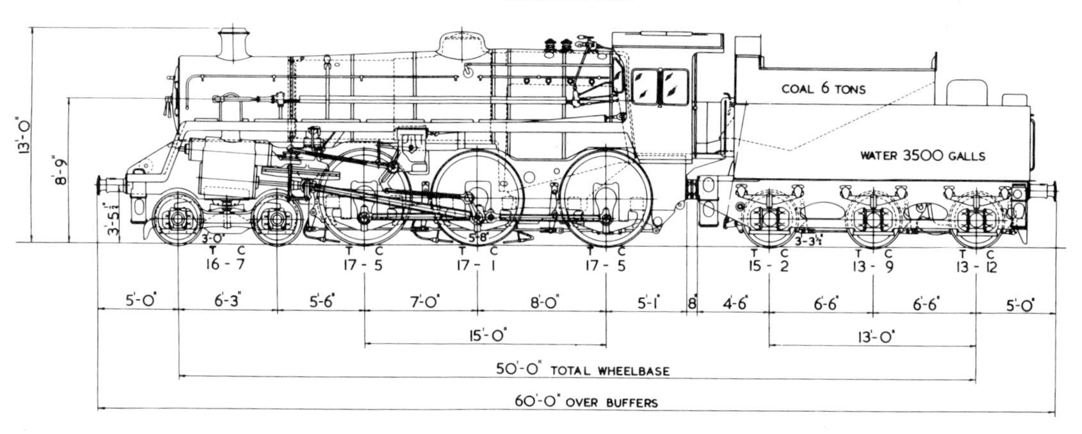

Above:
General arrangement of BR Standard 75000 Class 4 4-6-0 designed at Brighton, with BR2A tender.

Below:
Successor to the Stanier 'Black 5s', Standard Class 5 4-6-0 No 73116 *Iseult* approaches Wilton with an eastbound express on 10 August 1963. This was one of the Southern Region's 'Standard 5s' given names from withdrawn 'King Arthur' class locomotives. *A. Richardson*

Two 4-6-0 classes were included in the BR Standard types. The Class 5MT was related to the 'Black 5s' of the LMS through its boiler, which was similar to that of the 44800 series built by H. G. Ivatt. Its axle-load was 18ton. Class 4MT, with an axle-load of 17ton, was developed from the LMS Class 4 2-6-4T with the object of providing an engine with similar characteristics but capable of longer runs than a tank engine could manage. The firebox was of the same design as in the 2-6-4T but the boiler was 9in longer. In both 4-6-0s the fireboxes were Belpaire type. Class 5MT had roller bearings for the coupled and bogie axles but plain bearings were used on all axles of the Class 4 engine.

Building of the Class 5s was shared by Derby and Doncaster. Thirty locomotives built in 1956, Nos 73125-54, were fitted with Caprotti poppet valve gear similar to that which had given good results on No 71000 *Duke of Gloucester.* The drive to the camshafts was taken from return cranks on the middle pair of coupled wheels through a worm

Above left:
A close-up view of the Caprotti valve gear on Class 5 No 73144. *F. J. Saunders*

Left:
Class 4 4-6-0 No 75014 is seen near Cambridge with an evening parcels train to Bletchley. The locomotive is fitted with a single blastpipe and chimney. *M. Barratt*

Above:
Class 4 4-6-0 No 75075 stands at Nine Elms depot on Sunday 9 July 1967, the last day of steam operation on the Southern Region and the locomotive's final day in traffic. 75075 is fitted with a double blastpipe and chimney and coupled to a high sided BRIB tender. *J. Seddon*

gearbox and universally-jointed shafts. All the Class 4 engines were built at Swindon. Fifteen allocated to the Southern Region, Nos 75065-79, were fitted with double chimneys and blastpipes, and a number of others in the class were equipped similarly later. The Southern Region also had an allocation of 23 Class 5s, of which 20 were given names carried formerly by 'King Arthur' class 4-6-0s.

The '5MT' class went to all Regions of BR, but in greatest numbers to the LMR. Class 4MT was allocated in the main to the London Midland and Western Regions, but the final batch went to the Southern. The WR Class 4s had a long innings on the Central Wales line, working the 'Cambrian Coast Express' and finally displacing the 'Manors' which had worked there. Central Wales duties had been much in mind when the class was planned, as an area where more locomotive capacity was needed.

Standard 2-6-0s

Number series: 76000-76114
Cylinders: Two, 17.5in × 26in
Heating surface:
Tubes: 1,075sq ft
Firebox: 131sq ft
Superheater: 247sq ft
Total: 1,435sq ft
Grate area: 23sq ft
Boiler pressure: 225lb

Wheel arrangement: 2-6-0
Valve gear: Walschaerts
Driving wheel dia: 5ft 3in
TE at 85% pressure: 24,170lb
Weight: Loco: 59ton 2cwt
Tender: 42ton 3cwt
First loco built: December 1952
Last loco withdrawn: September 1968

* Refers to BR2 tender. Other tender types also used.

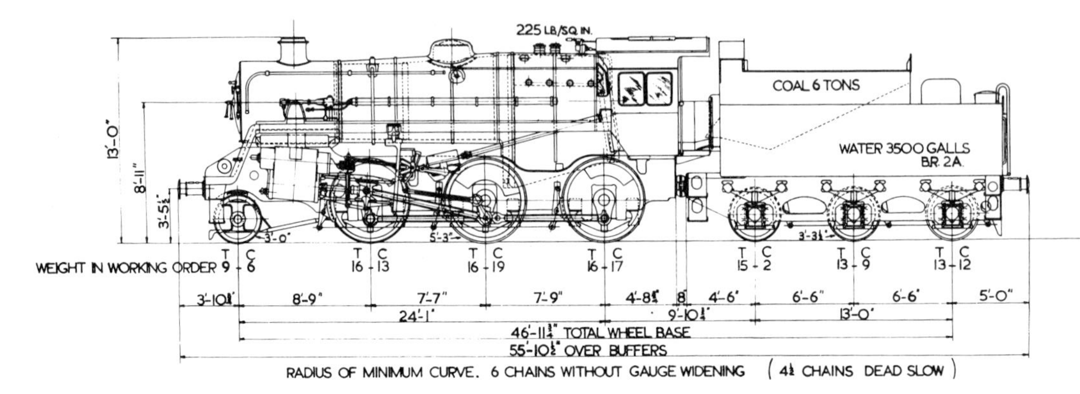

Number series: 77000-77019
Cylinders: Two, 17.5in × 26in
Heating surface:
Tubes: 923.54sq ft
Firebox: 118.42sq ft
Superheater: 184.5sq ft
Total: 1,226.46sq ft
Grate area: 20.35sq ft
Boiler pressure: 200lb/sq in

Wheel arrangement: 2-6-0
Valve gear: Walschaerts
Driving wheel dia: 5ft 3in
TE at 85% pressure: 21,490lb
Weight: Loco: 57ton 9cwt
Tender: 42ton 3cwt
First loco built: February 1954
Last loco withdrawn: June 1967

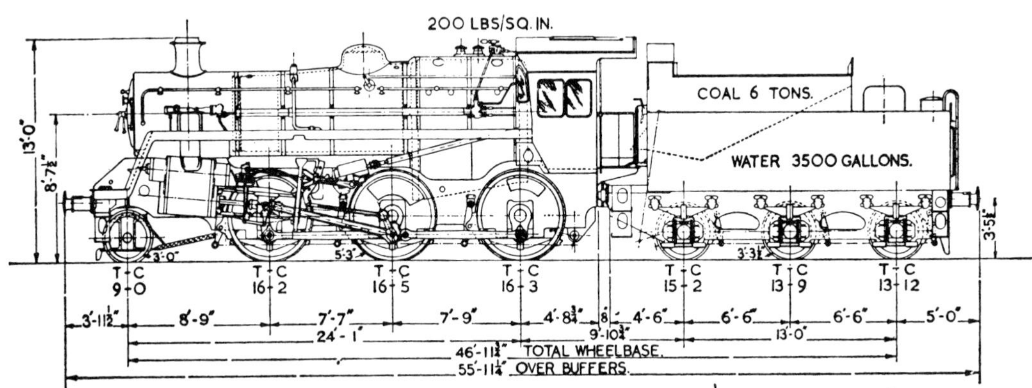

Number series: 78000-78064
Cylinders: Two, 16.5in × 24in
Heating surface:
Tubes: 924sq ft
Firebox: 101sq ft
Superheater: 124sq ft
Total: 1,149sq ft
Grate area: 17.5sq ft
Boiler pressure: 200lb/sq in
Wheel arrangement: 2-6-0
Valve gear: Walschaerts
Driving wheel dia: 5ft 0in
TE at 85% pressure: 18,515lb
Weight: Loco: 49ton 4cwt
Tender: 36ton 17cwt
First loco built: December 1952
Last loco withdrawn: May 1967

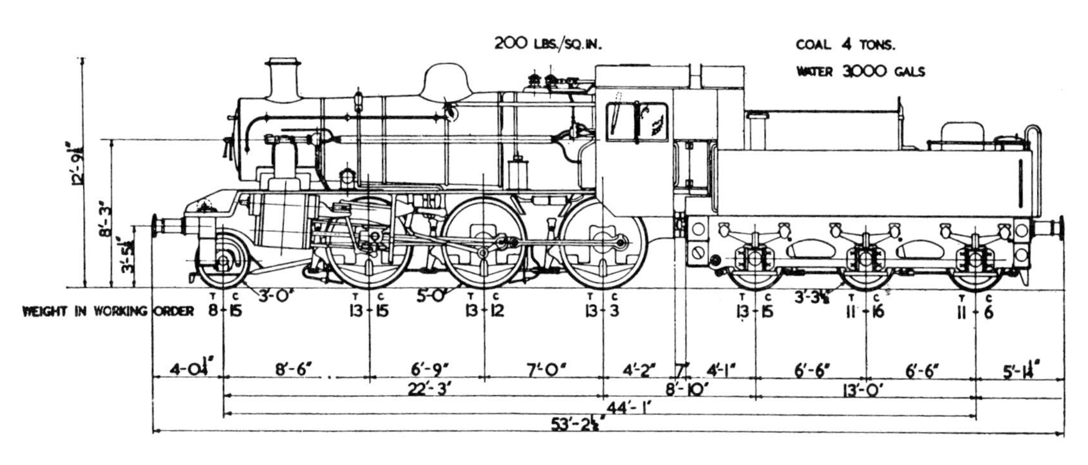

Top left:
General arrangement of BR Standard 76000 Class 4 2-6-0 designed at Doncaster, with BR2A tender.

Centre left:
General arrangement of BR Standard 77000 Class 3 2-6-0 designed at Swindon, with BR2A tender.

Left:
Class 4 2-6-0 No 76041 ambles through the Chilterns in charge of a GC section stopping train. This was the largest of the three BR standard 2-6-0 designs. *E. R. Wethersett/IAL*

Top:
A Blair Atholl-Perth stopping service near Dunkeld on 15 May 1954 is headed by Class 3 2-6-0 No 77008.
W. J. V. Anderson

Above:
General arrangement of BR Standard 78000 Class 2 2-6-0 designed at Derby, with BR3 tender.

Above:
Smallest of the BR Standard tender locomotives was the Class 2 2-6-0. No 78054 leaves Nethy Bridge on the Great North of Scotland line in September 1957, making for Boat of Garten. *W. J. V. Anderson*

The three BR Standard 2-6-0s were in power classes 4, 3 and 2MT. The Class 4MT engines were virtually a repeat of Ivatt's engines of 1947 for the LMS, but with standard fittings. Maximum axle-load was 16ton 19cwt. Class 3 was a similar engine but with a maximum axle-load of 16ton 5cwt so that it could work on lines from which the Class 4 2-6-0 was barred by its weight. For this reason it was fitted with a lighter boiler of the type used on several GWR tank engine classes. The Class 2 2-6-0 was again an adaptation of an Ivatt design for the LMS and followed tradition more closely in that the running plates were attached to the frames instead of to brackets from the boiler. Maximum axle-load was 13ton 15cwt.

Standard tank engines

Number series: 80000-80154
Cylinders: Two, 18in × 28in
Heating surface:
Tubes: 1,223sq ft
Firebox: 143sq ft
Superheater: 240sq ft
Total: 1,606sq ft
Grate area: 26.7sq ft
Boiler pressure: 225lb
Wheel arrangement: 2-6-4T
Valve gear: Walschaerts
Driving wheel dia: 5ft 8in
TE at 85% pressure: 25,515lb
Weight: 88ton 10cwt
First loco built: July 1951
Last loco withdrawn: July 1967

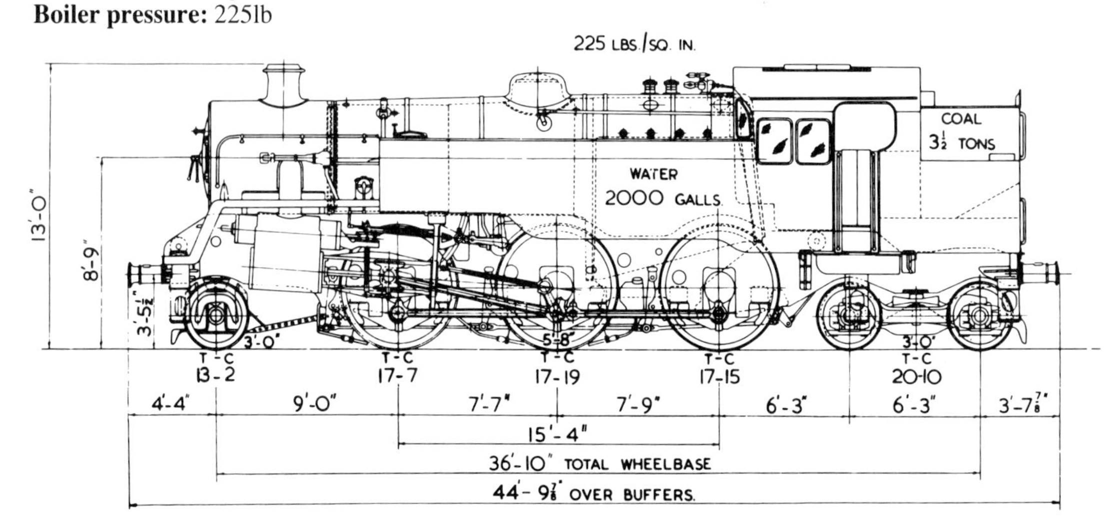

Number series: 82000-82044
Cylinders: Two, 17.5in × 26in
Heating surface:
Tubes: 923.54sq ft
Firebox: 118.42q ft
Superheater: 184.50sq ft
Total: 1,226.46sq ft
Grate area: 20.35sq ft
Boiler pressure: 200lb/sq in

Wheel arrangement: 2-6-2T
Valve gear: Walschaerts
Driving wheel dia: 5ft 3in
TE at 85% pressure: 21,490lb
Weight: 73ton 10cwt
First loco built: April 1952
Last loco withdrawn: July 1967

Below:
General arrangement of BR Standard 82000 Class 3 2-6-2T designed at Swindon.

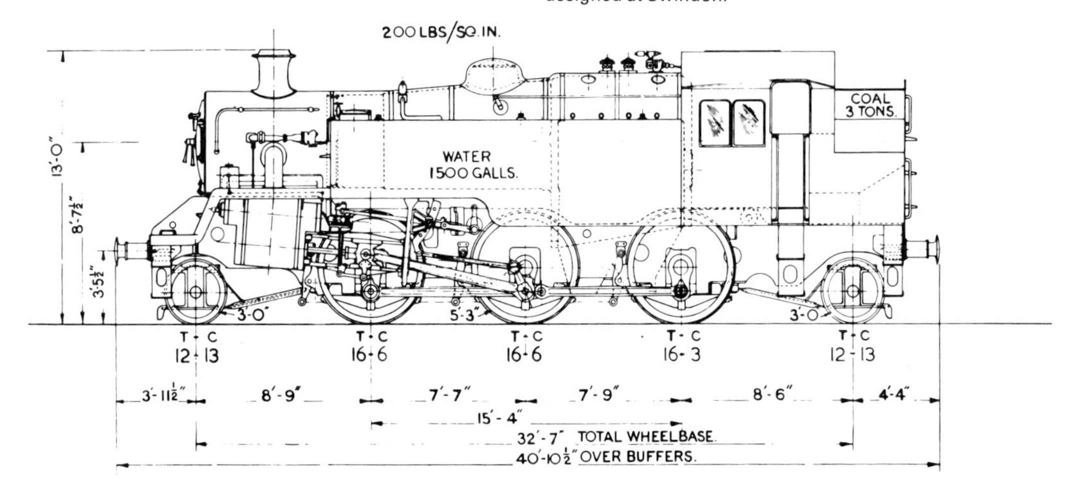

Number series: 84000-84029
Cylinders: Two, 16.5in × 24in
Heating surface:
Tubes: 924sq ft
Firebox: 101sq ft
Superheater: 124sq ft
Total: 1,149sq ft
Grate area: 17.5sq ft
Boiler pressure: 200lb/sq in

Wheel arrangement: 2-6-2T
Valve gear: Walschaerts
Driving wheel dia: 5ft 0in
TE at 85% pressure: 18,515lb
Weight: 63ton 5cwt
First loco built: July 1953
Last loco withdrawn: January 1966

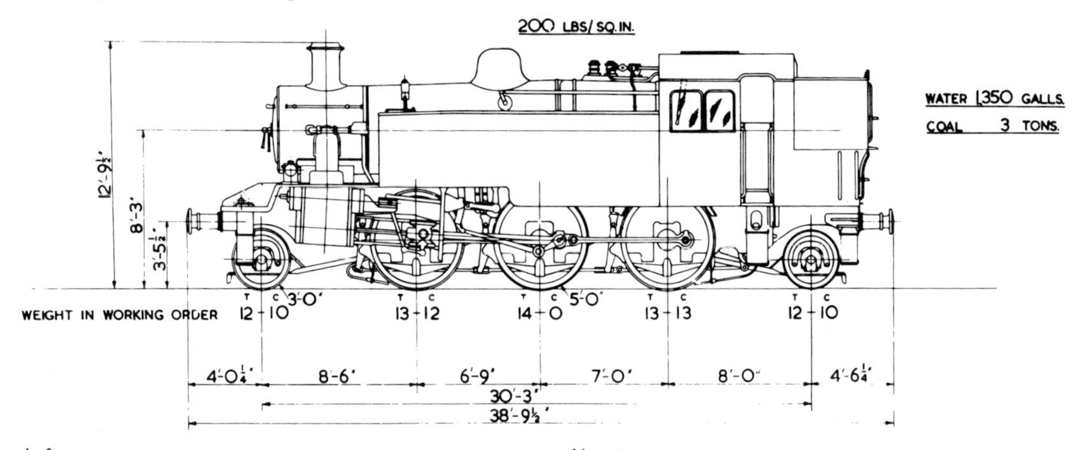

Left:
General arrangement of BR Standard 80000 Class 4 2-6-4T designed at Brighton.

Above:
General arrangement of BR Standard 84000 Class 2 2-6-2T designed at Derby.

80045

82001

84001
84001

Left:
The Standard Class 4 2-6-4T was developed from the Fairburn LMS tank locomotive, with boiler pressure raised to 225lb/sq in. No 80045 wheels a local down the Midland main line near Mill Hill on 5 September 1953. *E. R. Wethersett/IAL*

Centre left:
The intermediate size Standard tank design was the Class 3 2-6-2T, represented here by No 82001 working a Stratford-upon-Avon–Birmingham stopping train on 16 May 1952. *T. Williams*

Bottom left:
The Class 2 2-6-2T was popularly known as a 'Mickey Mouse'. No 84001 of this class passes Crewe North Junction on a push-pull working to Northwich. This was a tank version of the 78000 2-6-0 tender locomotive.
P. Ransome-Wallis

The standard tank engines comprised one class with the 2-6-4 and two with the 2-6-2 wheel arrangements. All were reminiscent in appearance and design of the Ivatt/Fairburn period on the LMS. Boilers in the 2-6-4T and Class 2 2-6-2T were based on the corresponding LMS types but the Class 3 2-6-2T carried a boiler similar to that of the Great Western 51XX series tank engines to reduce the axle load. Maximum weight on the coupled wheels in Class 3 was 16ton 6cwt compared with 17ton 19cwt in Class 4. The Class 2 was a still lighter engine with a maximum axle-load of 14ton.

All three classes were intended for suburban, outer surburban and local passenger duties. They began to come out from the works in the latter half of 1951. Construction of Class 4 was shared between Derby, Brighton and Doncaster; Class 3 came from Swindon, and Class 2 from Darlington. In 1953 the process of changing to diesel multiple-unit trains for local services began in certain areas of the country and the report of the British Transport Commission said that the year 'marked the beginning of a very large programme of multiple-unit diesel car construction'. It added the comment that 'diesel multiple-unit sets offer many advantages of electrification including cleanliness, good acceleration, and ability to turn round quickly at terminals'. It could hardly have been stated more plainly that the local steam train was on the way out while the new tank locomotives were still coming in.

Class 9F 2-10-0

Number series: 92000-92250
Cylinders: Two, 20in × 28in
Heating surface:
Tubes: 1,836sq ft
Firebox: 179sq ft
Superheater: 535sq ft
Total: 2,550sq ft
Grate area: 40.2sq ft
Boiler pressure: 250lb/sq in

Wheel arrangement: 2-10-0
Valve gear: Walschaerts
Driving wheel dia: 5ft 0in
TE at 85% pressure: 39,667lb
Weight: Loco: 86ton 14cwt
Tender: 51ton 5cwt*
First loco built: January 1954
Last loco withdrawn: June 1968

Note: Nos 92020-92029 fitted with Crosti boiler. Weight: 90 ton 4 cwt
* Refers to BR1B tender. Other tender types also used.

Below:
General arrangement of BR Standard 92000 Class 9F 2-10-0 designed at Brighton, with BR1G tender.

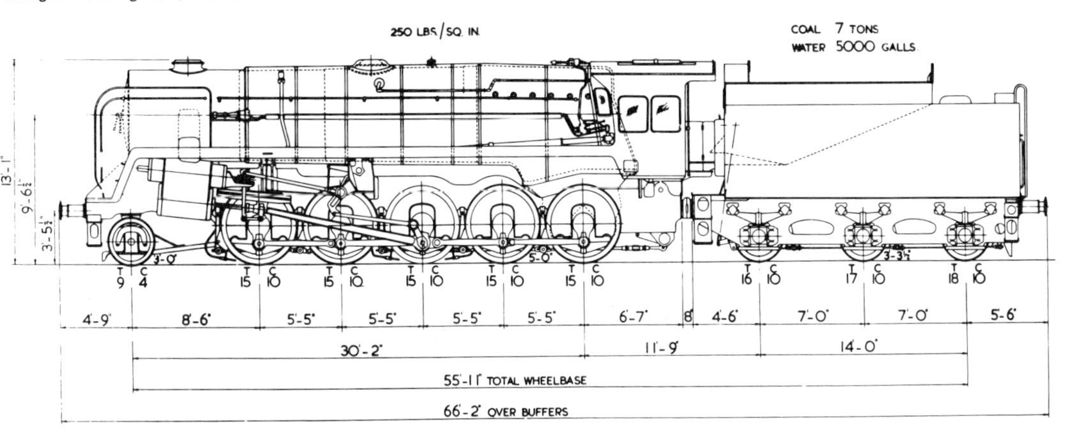

Until World War 2, ten-coupled locomotives in Great Britain had been confined to two 'one-off' types – the Great Eastern 'Decapod' built to fight off pressure for electrification out of Liverpool Street by showing that steam could match the acceleration of an EMU; and the Midland Railway's banking locomotive for the Lickey Incline. In 1944, however, a 2-10-0 version of the War Department's 'Austerity' 2-8-0 was built in order to carry a larger boiler although having approximately the same tractive power. The same wheel arrangment was chosen for the freight locomotive in the BR Standard range. This became the most numerous of the Standard classes, totalling 251 engines, of which 178 were built at Crewe and 73 at Swindon. The last of the Swindon batch, No 92220 *Evening Star*, was the last steam locomotive built for British Railways. It was named at Swindon with appropriate ceremony on 18 March 1960 and is preserved today by the National Railway Museum.

Although the class was given a freight classification, it was intended to cover mixed traffic duties and was given coupled wheels of 5ft dia as compared with the 4ft 8½in dia wheels of the 'Austerities'. Some fast runs on passenger duties were recorded in the closing years of steam when drivers succumbed more often to the temptation to 'have a go', and there is a well-authenticated record of 90mph. The engines were built with the attention to easy accessibility and straightforward maintenance and preparation prescribed for all the Standard classes, but they had plain bearings on all axles. The boiler, similar to that of the 'Britannias', was 1ft 9in shorter between tubeplates; the firebox was longer and shallower to clear the rear pair of coupled wheels.

The locomotives were the subject of several experiments. Nos 92020-29 built in 1952 were fitted with Crosti boilers. This was a twin-drum arrangement with the steam-raising boiler perched on top of a feedwater heating drum, a layout clearly visible in a smokebox view of the locomotive. Hot gases in the smokebox were led back through 90 tubes in the drum to a chimney in front of the cab, on the right-hand side of the locomotive. The chimney in the conventional position on the smokebox served only for the escape of smoke while lighting-up.

The exhaust steam followed a similar backward path in pipes on each side of the locomotive, leading to a blast chamber at the base of the rear chimney. A proportion of the steam was diverted through a steam jacket round part of the feedwater drum to help with the preheating. Expected economies were not achieved, however, and smoke and steam swirling round the cab made the engines unpopular. In 1959 No 92026 was converted to a normal exhaust arrangement with the feedwater heating system out of action, and the other nine Crosti engines were treated similarly. They remained in service until 1967, still 'Crostis' in form but not in fact.

Mechanical stokers were fitted to three engines built in 1958, Nos 92165-7, but although the rate of evaporation was higher than possible with hand firing, the gain was cancelled by the steam consumed by the stoker equipment. In 1962 the stokers were removed.

Left:
A Class 9F 2-10-0 in action. Laira allocated No 92223 storms out of Newton Abbot with a Tavistock Junction-Avonmouth express freight on 6 October 1959. This was a most successful design, although dieselisation resulted in ridiculously short working lives for the '9Fs'. *D. S. Fish*

Below:
This view of Franco Crosti boilered '9F' No 92029 passing through Bedford with an up freight shows the feedwater heating drum located below the boiler. Note the chimney located beside the boiler behind smoke deflector, the conventional chimney being used only for lighting up.
S. Creer

Trials of a double blastpipe and double chimney on No 92178 in 1957 led to all engines from No 92183 being equipped in this way when built, and some earlier ones being converted similarly. A Giesl exhaust system was fitted to No 92250 in December 1958. After trials on the Rugby test plant the engine was returned to regular service on the Western Region. In this system the exhaust was expelled through seven nozzles arranged in line, so that the chimney was long and narrow. There were high hopes in some quarters that the improvement of the draught would bring a renaissance of the steam locomotive. Others were less sanguine. R. C. Bond commented (Bond, R. C. *A Lifetime with Locomotives.* Goose & Son 1975):

'When I was Chief Mechanical Engineer I had declined to try the special design of blastpipe. With steam on the way out, expenditure thereon could not be justified in my opinion by any economy which might accrue for a short time only on our modern locomotives. Pressure was however later applied by the back door. Instructions were given that a trial had to be undertaken. The resulting tests carried out at Rugby on standard 2-10-0 locomotives were entirely as we had predicted but it took some time and much patience to shake off our pursuers.'

3 Early Diesel and Gas Turbine Designs

Nos 10000 and 10001

Number series: 10000, 10001
Engine: English Electric 16SVT
Cylinders: Sixteen, 10in × 12in
Rating: 1,600hp at 750rpm
Transmission: Six nose-suspended traction motors
Maximum speed: 93mph

Wheel arrangement: Co-Co
Driving wheel dia: 3ft 6in
Continuous TE: 15,000lb
Maximum TE: 41,400lb
Weight: 127ton 13cwt
First loco built: December 1947
Last loco withdrawn: March 1966

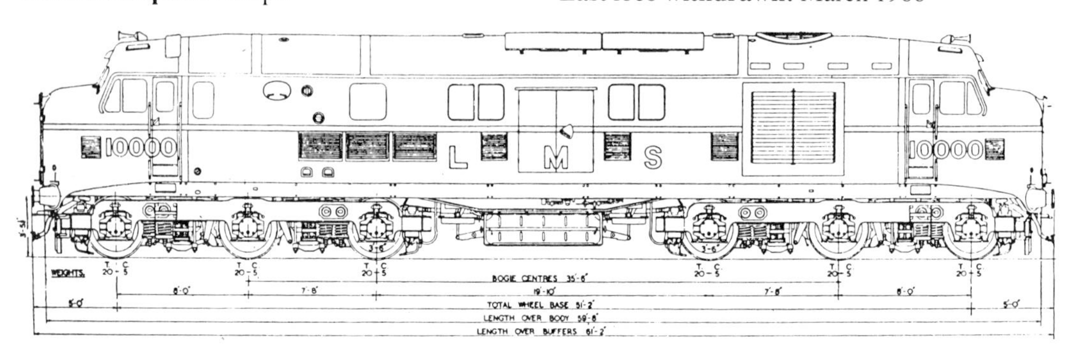

Above:
General arrangement of diesel-electric Co-Co Nos 10000/1.

With nationalisation looming, the London Midland & Scottish Railway was determined the parentage of British Railways' first main line diesel-electric locomotives should not be forgotten. They were an LMS project, and No 10000 was driven out of Derby Works just under two months before BR came into being on 1 January 1948. To make sure that credit went where it was due the letters 'LMS'

Below:
The main line diesel makes its appearance in the shape of LMS-built Co-Co No 10000. Many of British Railways' later diesel locomotives were directly descended from this unit and its twin No 10001, with successive developments of the English Electric 16SVT engine. *E. R. Wethersett/IAL*

were cast into the footplating. No 10000's 'twin', 10001, began its trials on 5 July 1948. The locomotives could work in multiple as a pair aggregating 3,200hp.

Power equipment was supplied by English Electric. The prime mover was the 16-cylinder 16SVT engine, first of a famous range which has improved in output per cylinder and power-to-weight ratio over the years. Wheel arrangement was Co-Co, with bogies of special design in which the weight on the swing bolsters was carried on sliding surfaces, the pivot dealing only with traction and braking forces. There were two bolsters per bogie, coupled by a connecting member in which the pivot was situated. Laminated springs carried the bolsters, and the primary suspension was by coil springs which transmitted the weight to equalising beams bearing on top of the axleboxes. On the LMR the locomotives worked on Anglo-Scottish services, mostly as a pair, and singly on services between Euston and the northwest. In the 1950s they had a spell on the Southern Region but finished their career back on the LMR.

The pair achieved a record performance while working between Euston and Glasgow in 1949, making the round trip in a day, with a mileage of approximately 810 miles including running to and from the sheds. Power was controlled by an eight-notch system giving engine speeds of 450, 620 and 750rpm and various degrees of generator excitation.

No 10100

Number series: 10100
Engines: Four Paxman 12RPH
Cylinders: Twelve 7in × 7.75in
Rating: 500hp at 1,500rpm
Transmission: Fell patent differential drive and fluid couplings
Maximum speed: 72mph
Wheel arrangement: 4-8-4
Driving wheel dia: 4ft 3in
Maximum TE: 29,400lb
Weight: 120ton
Loco built: January 1951
Loco withdrawn: December 1958

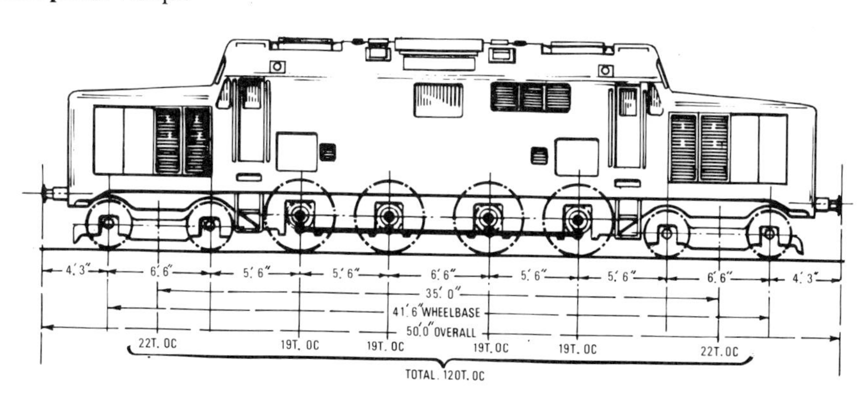

Above:
General arrangement of Fell diesel 4-8-4 No 10100.

An unusual experiment in applying mechanical transmission to a powerful main line diesel locomotive was begun in 1948 when BR's Derby Works started work on a 2,000hp locomotive designed for the transmission system developed by Lt-Col L. F. R. Fell. The Fell locomotive was powered by four Paxman engines of 500hp which drove the two intermediate axles of a four-axle coupled wheelbase through a common gearbox. Each engine was connected to the gearbox by a fluid coupling, and the drive was taken through a train of differential gears.

With the four engines idling and their couplings empty of oil, one coupling was filled and its engine accelerated to start a train. This gave a 'first gear' condition with high torque at low speed. At a predetermined speed the coupling of engine No 2 was filled, the driver operating a small trigger, and that engine accelerated. With a second differential gear now operating, the output shaft was driven faster as if a higher gear had been engaged, and there was a similar effect as engines 3 and 4 were brought in, the final condition being equivalent to four engines transmitting power through a direct drive. Engine No 1 worked alone from 0 to 6mph, Nos 1 and 2 from 6 to 17mph, Nos 1, 2 and 3 from 17 to 24mph, and all four engines from 24 to 78mph.

Above:
The four-engined Fell diesel-mechanical locomotive No 10100 pulls out of Loughborough for St Pancras with a train for Derby on 20 March 1952 during a short period of passenger work on the Midland main line. *B. S. Jennings*

The locomotive had the falling tractive effort/speed characteristic required for traction and there were no interruptions of effort by gear changes. The final drive to the wheels of the two intermediate axles from two quill shafts was by means of drive arms on the shafts acting on the driving wheel spokes through rubber blocks. All driving wheels were coupled as in normal steam practice, the wheel arrangement being 4-8-4. The engines were in the 'nose' ends, two side by side in each, arranged longitudinally. In the main body of the locomotive were the fluid couplings, main gearbox, two 150hp auxiliary diesels driving pressure-chargers for the main engines, and two train heating boilers.

No 10100 emerged from Derby in January 1951 and was soon working St Pancras-Manchester trains but with frequent return visits to works for adjustment. It was purchased by BR in 1955 and tested on the Settle-Carlisle line, after which the locomotive worked various passenger and freight turns on the Midland lines. Serious damage was inflicted when a train heating boiler caught fire in Manchester Central in 1958 and the locomotive was withdrawn, never to return to duty. It was broken up in 1960.

The Southern Main Line Diesels

Number series: 10201, 10202
Engine: English Electric 16SVT
Cylinders: Sixteen, 10in × 12in
Rating: 1,750hp at 750rpm
Transmission: Six axle-hung, nose-suspended traction motors
Maximum speed: 90mph
Wheel arrangement: 1Co-Co1
Driving wheel dia: 3ft 7in
Continuous TE: 21,700lb at 24.5mph
Maximum TE: 48,000lb
Weight: 135ton
First loco built: November 1950
Both locos withdrawn: December 1963

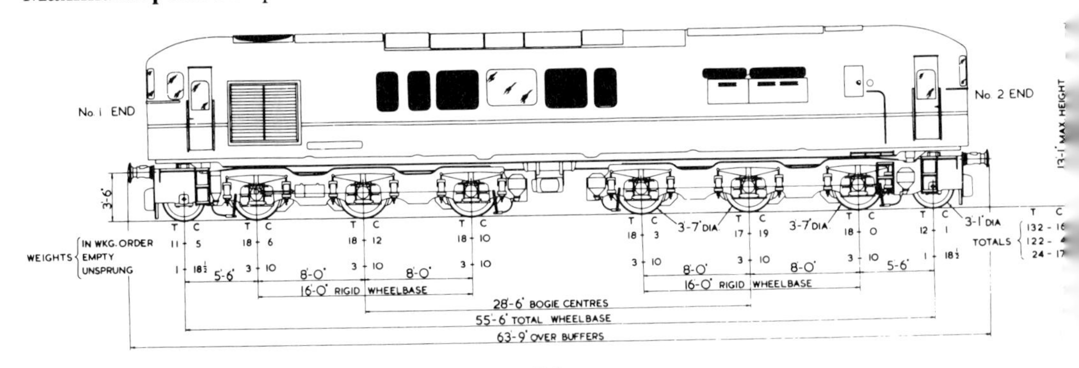

Number series: 10203
Engine: English Electric 16SVT MkII
Cylinders: Sixteen, 10in × 12in
Rating: 2,000hp at 850rpm
Transmission: Six axle-hung, nose-suspended traction motors
Maximum speed: 90mph

Wheel arrangement: 1Co-Co1
Driving wheel dia: 3ft 7in
Continuous TE: 30,000lb at 19mph
Maximum TE: 50,000lb
Weight: 132ton
Loco built: March 1954
Loco withdrawn: December 1963

'lans for a pilot scheme of main line diesel traction n the Southern Railway originated in 1946 but the vork was held up and the first of three locomotives vas not completed until 1951. No 10201, designed nd built at Ashford, was a 1Co-Co1 powered by an nglish Electric 16SVT engine similar to that in the MR diesels 10000/01. In the first two Southern ocomotives, however, its rating at 750rpm was iven as 1,750hp. The bogies were similar to those the Southern's Co-Co electric locomotives but ith an additional carrying axle. This was in the orm of a pony truck attached to the bogie by two ort links ahead of the axle and anchored on the uffer beam. Side play was controlled by springs at the rear. The bogies were pivoted directly from the main frame in segmental bearings which prevented tilting and restricted weight transfer at high tractive efforts. This arrangement was a legacy of O. V. S. Bulleid who had left British Railways in 1949.

The main generator supplied three series pairs of axle-hung traction motors. Maximum outputs were 900V and 3,000A, and field weakening enabled the full engine horsepower to be used up to 80mph. Originally there was one weak-field step but an intermediate step was added later. There was also a change in gear ratio from 21:52 to 17:65.

In 1952 the second locomotive in the class, No 10202, underwent trials with a dynamometer car while working between Waterloo and Exeter. At that time the locomotive had an eight-notch controller and it was found that in the high power, high speed area the control was not well balanced between the notches; in particular there was a big gap in power between notches 7 and 8. Dynamometer charts showed surges in tractive effort in moving from notch to notch, and also when

ft:
eneral arrangement of diesel-electric 1 Co-Co 1 No 10203.

bove:
outhern Region 1,750hp diesel-electric No 10202 at work the London Midland Region. The locomotive is leaving ewe with an express for Euston on 21 July 1962.
Haresnape

Above:
The third Southern main line diesel, No 10203 of 2,000hp is on its home ground near Andover with the former GWR Swindon dynamometer car at the head of its train in July 1955. *G. Wheeler*

taking the two weak-field steps at 31 and 46mph, although less pronounced than with the original single weak-field step at 46mph.

Information from the tests of No 10202 formed the basis of certain modifications in the design of the third locomotive, No 10203, which came out in 1954. A third weak-field step was introduced and control of engine speed was made continuous. The eight-step control used in Nos 10201/2 was adjusted to avoid critical speeds at which vibrations would be set up in the engine crankshaft. With progress in crankshaft design and damping arrangements critical speeds were shifted outside the engine operating range, and the continuous control first seen on BR in No 10203 and the prototype 'Deltic' has since become general. No 10203 had an uprated 16SVT engine, the 16SVT/II, giving 2,000hp at 850rpm.

No 10800

Number series: 10800
Engine: Paxman 16RPHXL
Cylinders: Sixteen
Rating: 827hp at 1,250rpm
Transmission: Four nose-suspended traction motors
Maximum speed: 70mph
Wheel arrangement: Bo-Bo
Wheel dia: 3ft 6in
Maximum TE: 34,500lb
Weight: 69ton 16cwt
Loco built: May 1950
Loco withdrawn: August 1959

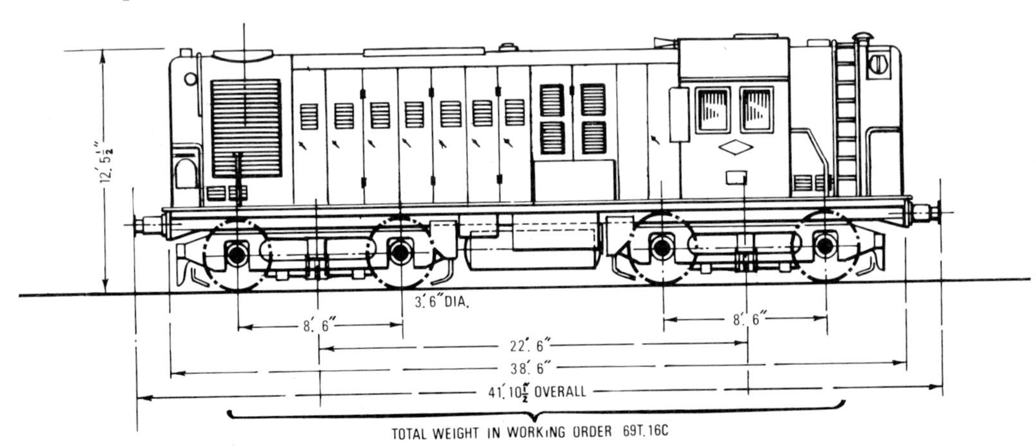

The LMS diesel-electric programme comprised two main line Co-Co locomotives (BR Nos 10000/01) and a Bo-Bo of 827hp for secondary services. The Bo-Bo, built by the North British Locomotive Co Ltd, was not completed until 1950. After trial running in Scotland it was handed over to the London Midland Region with the number 10800. Later years took it to the Southern, and then to the Birmingham-Peterborough route. The engine was the Paxman 16RPHXL with a rating of 827hp at 1,250rpm. Electrical equipment was by BTH. No 10800 remained in active service until 1959, when locomotives ordered under the modernisation plan were working in increasing numbers. They included two mixed traffic Bo-Bo designs with 16-cylinder Paxman engines (Classes 15 and 16) which can be considered as derivatives of the LMS project. After withdrawal, No 10800 was saved from scrapping by becoming a research locomotive in a joint venture by BR and Brush to examine the possibilities of squirrel-cage induction motors for traction. The original engine-generator set was replaced by a Bristol-Siddeley-Maybach MD655 coupled to a brushless alternator. After rectification, the alternator output was converted into three-phase ac at variable frequency by inverter circuits. Following the Brush tradition of bird names, the project was given the name 'Hawk'. This was an early venture in a direction that has seen much development in recent years, both for diesel-electric and 'straight' electric locomotives. At the time, however, the thyristors and associated circuits necessary for the scheme had not reached a sufficiently advanced stage to make it economically attractive and reliable. Trial running on the old GC main line between Leicester and Nottingham began in April 1965, and by the beginning of 1966 the locomotive had undergone tests at Rugby preparatory to further running on the GC section, but still on a trial basis. As this was very much a pilot scheme, frequent modifications were made to the inverter components and circuitry and in 1968 the project came to a halt as finance ran out. It was not resumed and the locomotive was finally broken up in 1972. Useful experience had been gained of alternators for diesel traction but was first put to practical use in locomotives with rectifiers and dc motors. The inverter-fed squirrel-cage motor did not become a practical proposition until nearly ten years had elapsed after the 'Hawk' project was abandoned.

Left:
General arrangement of diesel-electric Bo-Bo No 10800.

Above:
The lesser-known third main line diesel ordered by the LMS, although not delivered until after nationalisation was the Paxman engined No 10800, seen at Brighton in September 1952. *P. F. Winding/IA Library Collection*

No 11001

Number: 11001
Engine: Paxman V-type
Cylinders: Twelve
Rating: 500hp
Transmission: Three-speed gearbox and fluid coupling
Maximum speed: 43.5mph

Wheel arrangement: 0-6-0DM
Driving wheel dia: 4ft 6in
Maximum TE: 33,000lb
Weight: 49ton 9cwt
Loco built: 1949
Loco withdrawn: August 1959

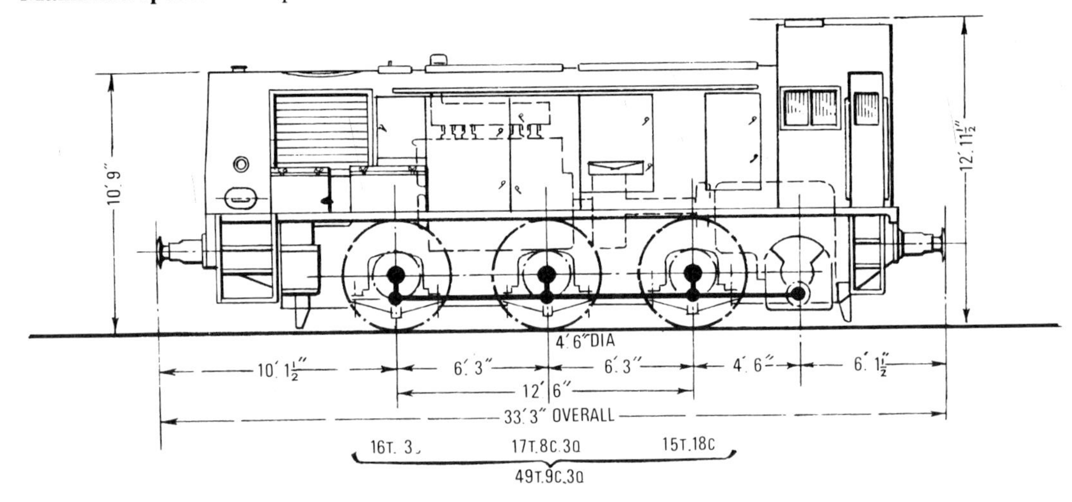

Above:
General arrangement of diesel-mechanical 0-6-0 No 11001.

Although designed by the Southern Railway, due to delays in construction the locomotive did not appear from Ashford Works until well into British Railways days. It was intended for freight trip working and heavy shunting duties. The Bulleid influence in the design is clear, particularly in the Boxpok wheels. Although more powerful than contemporary diesel shunter designs, 11001 proved in service to be an unfortunate compromise between shunting and train working duties and was not totally successful in either role.

Below:
The unique Southern Region shunting locomotive No 11001, designed by O.V. Bulleid was powered by a 500hp Paxman engine. Its distinctive BFB Boxpok wheels can clearly be seen. *British Rail SR*

Western Region Gas Turbines

In the 1950s there was considerable interest in the gas turbine as an alternative to the diesel engine for railway traction. The turbine has some of the advantages of the diesel without the complication of converting reciprocating to rotary motion, added to which it can burn low-grade fuel and has a lower consumption of lubricating oil. In thermal efficiency, however, the diesel engine has a slight lead.

In a gas turbine system, air is first compressed and then passes to combustion chambers where fuel is injected and burned. The stream of hot gases acts on turbine blades on a shaft coupled to the compressor and also to the machine to be driven. There is a surplus of power at the turbine shaft because the work available from expansion of the hot gases is greater than that required to compress the air. In most railway gas turbine applications, the surplus power has been used to drive an electrical generator.

Number: 18000
Engine: Gas turbine of 5,800rpm
Rating: 2,500hp
Transmission: Four fully springborne traction motors
Maximum speed: 90mph
Driving wheel dia: 4ft 0½in
Wheel arrangement: A1A-A1A
Continuous TE: 31,500lb at 21
Maximum TE: 60,000lb
Weight: 115ton 3cwt
Loco built: 1949
Loco withdrawn: December 1960

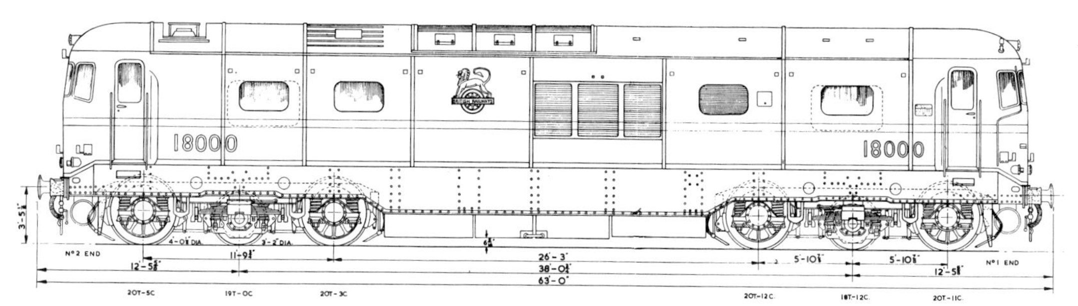

Above:
General arrangement of Western Region gas turbine A1A-A1A No 18000. *R. S. Carter*

Two gas turbine locomotives were taken into BR stock, both on the Western Region. First of these was No 18000, built by Brown-Boveri and the Swiss Locomotive Works. After trials in Switzerland, the locomotive arrived in Britain on 3 February 1950. At that time a gas turbine locomotive could show an advantage over a diesel

Below:
Swiss-built gas turbine locomotive No 18000 is seen near Corsham on the 12 noon Bristol-Paddington express on 11 May 1951. *G. J. Jefferson*

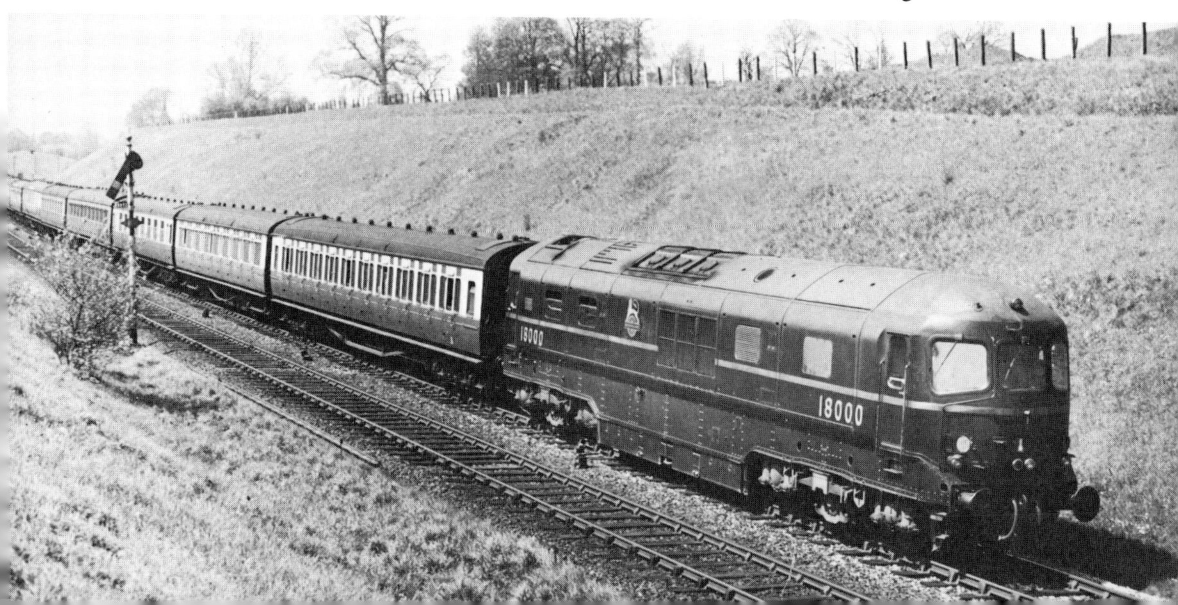

in size and weight. No 18000, weighing 115ton 3cwt and measuring 63ft overall, produced 2,500hp. The nearest diesel equivalent on BR at the time was the combination of Nos 10000 and 10001, giving 3,200hp for a total weight of 243ton and an overall length of 122ft 4in.

In No 18000 the air from the compressor passed through a heat exchanger before entering the combustion chamber, gaining heat from the turbine exhaust gases and so improving efficiency by reducing the amount of heat to be added by the fuel. In the compressor the air was compressed to about 45lb/sq in. A large proportion of the air, however, by-passed the compressor to reduce the temperature of the gases issuing from the combustion chamber. Air for the combustion chamber was raised to a temperature of about 500°F (260°C) in the heat exchanger, while the temperature in the combustion zone was about 3,300°F (1,656°C) but the cool by-pass air lowered the temperature of the gases leaving the chamber to about 1,100°F (433°C). The turbine ran at 5,800rpm and was coupled through reduction gears to the traction generator, which was driven at 875rpm. An auxiliary diesel-generator set supplied dc for generator excitation, auxiliaries and battery charging. The output from this set could be connected to two of the four traction motors for driving the locomotive for running light.

Wheel arrangement was A1A-A1A. In the SLM bogies all articulations with the body for controlling lateral and longitudinal motions were rubber-bushed. Motor torque was transmitted through Brown-Boveri spring drives, anticipating some of the prototype ac electric locomotives of later years.

Number: 18100
Engine: Gas turbine of 7,000rpm
Rating: 3,000hp
Transmission: Six nose-suspended traction motors
Maximum speed: 90mph
Driving wheel dia: 3ft 8in
Wheel arrangement: Co-Co
Continuous TE: 30,000lb
Maximum TE: 60,000lb
Weight: 129ton 10cwt
Loco built: December 1951
Loco withdrawn: January 1958

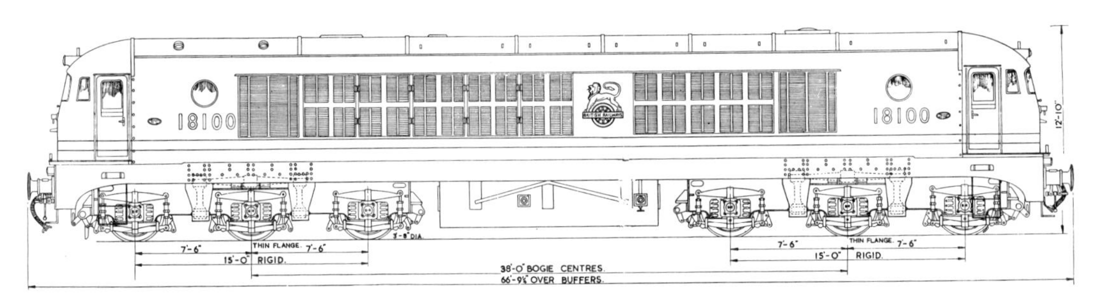

Above:
General arrangement of Western Region gas turbine Co-Co No 18100. *R. S. Carter*

The Western Region's second gas turbine locomotive was No 18100, built for the railway by the Metropolitan-Vickers Electrical Co Ltd and intended for hauling the Region's heaviest passenger trains, particularly between London and Plymouth, at speeds up to 90mph. This was a 3,000hp Co-Co powered by a 7,000rpm gas turbine without heat-exchanger. It was claimed that the combined thermal efficiency of the turbine and compressor had been improved to yield the same overall efficiency as in No 18000. Omission of the heat exchanger resulted in a gas turbine plant of reduced size and weight and allowed a unit of increased power to be installed. The turbine was direct-coupled to the compressor, which was coupled in turn to a reduction gear with two output shafts running at 1,600rpm. There were three traction generators, each supplying two traction motors. One output shaft drove two traction generators, while the other drove the third, together with an auxiliary generator and exciter. The combustion chamber consisted of six flame tubes arranged round the main shaft between the compressor and the five-stage turbine.

Traction motors were axle-hung. The bogies had no bolsters, the body being carried by swing links from the bogie frame, which were attached at their lower ends to support brackets extending downward from the body and passing outside the bogie frames, two on each side of each bogie. The links had rubber resilient joints to permit controlled swing bolster action and pivoting. Traction and braking forces were taken by the pivot kingpins which were connected with the bogie cross-stays by parallel motion linkages fitted with universal joints.

Above:
The Western Region's second gas turbine locomotive was No 18100, built by Metropolitan-Vickers. On 5 April 1952 it heads the down 'Merchant Venturer' (Paddington-Bristol) past Iver. *C. R. L. Coles*

No 18100 was handed over to the Western Region early in 1952. Although with the spread of diesel traction on the WR the locomotive had long periods out of use it was not officially withdrawn until 1 January 1958. It was then converted into an ac electric locomotive for driver training in preparation for the first stages of the LMR electrification from Manchester and Liverpool to Crewe. The locomotive was first renumbered E1000, and in 1959 was renumbered E2001. After intermittent use for training and test purposes it was withdrawn in 1968 and eventually sold for scrap in 1972.

4 British Railways Diesel Locomotives

It would not be feasible within the confines of this work to cover the numerous different designs of diesel shunter which appeared during the 1940s and 1950s. Instead this book gives an outline of those generally more successful designs which survived to be given TOPS class numbers. The various precursors to the standard Class 08 shunter are not dealt with, also on grounds of space. A comprehensive coverage of British Rail diesel shunting locomotives is provided by *British Rail Fleet Survey No 7, Diesel Shunters* (Ian Allan Ltd, 1984).

Class: 01 0-4-0DM
Builder: A. Barclay
Engine: Gardner 6L3
Rating: 153hp at 1,200rpm

Nos D2953-D2956†
Transmission: Mechanical
First loco built: January 1956
Last loco withdrawn: March 1981

† D2954-D2955 later renumbered 01.001 and 01.002.

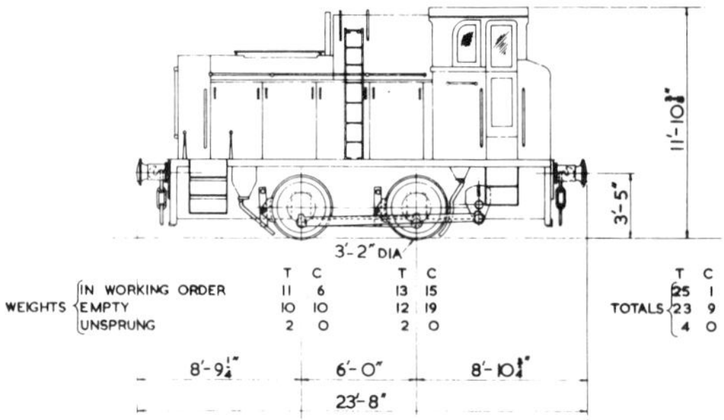

Class: 02 0-4-0DH
Builder: Yorks Engine Co
Engine: Rolls Royce C6NFL
Rating: 179hp at 1,800rpm

Nos D2850-D2869†
Transmission: Hydraulic
First loco built: September 1960
Last loco withdrawn: June 1975

† Later renumbered 02.002-02.004.

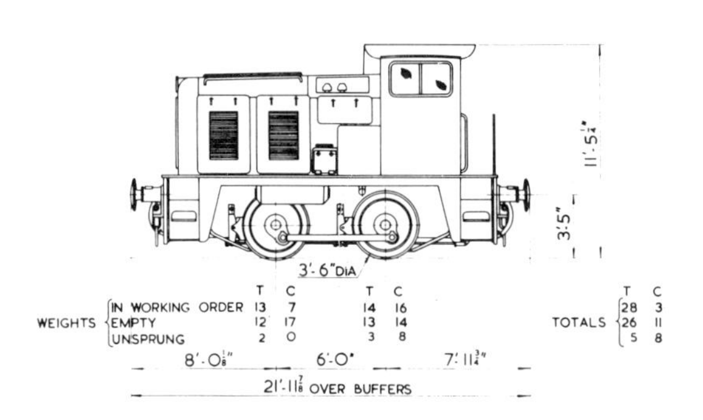

Class: 03 0-6-0DM
Builder: British Railways
Engine: Gardner 8L3
Rating: 204hp at 1,200rpm

Nos D2000-D2199, D2372-D2399†
Transmission: Mechanical
First loco built: December 1957

† Later renumbered 03.004-03.382

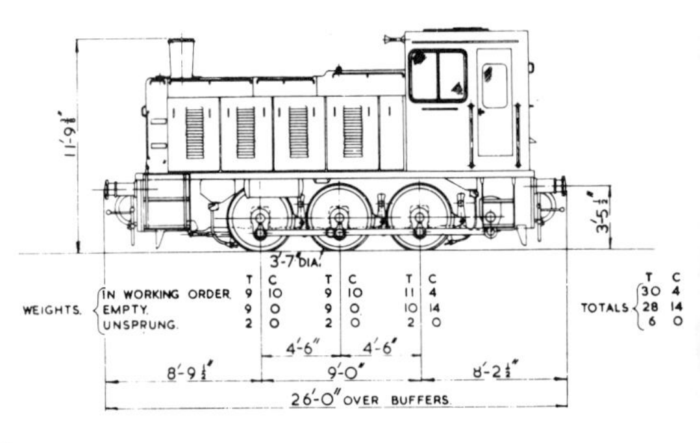

Class 04 0-6-0DM
Builder: Drewry Car Co
Engine: Gardner 8L3
Rating: 204hp at 1,200rpm

Nos D2200-D2340
Transmission: Mechanical
First loco built: May 1952
Last loco withdrawn: May 1972

Below left:
General arrangement of 153hp Class 01 diesel-mechanical 0-4-0.

Centre left:
General arrangement of 179hp Class 02 diesel-hydraulic 0-4-0.

Bottom left:
General arrangement of 204hp Class 03 diesel-mechanical 0-6-0.

Below:
Most successful and most numerous of the various designs of small diesel shunter built for British Railways was the BR built 0-6-0DM introduced in 1957 and later classified Class 03. No D2183 is seen here outside Swindon works.

Class 05 0-6-0DM
Builder: Hunslet
Engine: Gardner 8L3
Rating: 204hp at 1,200rpm

Nos D2550-D2618†
Transmission: Mechanical
First loco built: October 1955
Last loco withdrawn: January 1981

† D2554 renumbered 05.001 and later departmental stock 97803

Class 06 0-4-0DM
Builder: A. Barclay
Engine: Gardner 8L3
Rating: 204hp at 1,200rpm

Nos D2410-D2444†
Transmission: Mechanical
First loco built: June 1958
Last loco withdrawn: September 1981

† Later renumbered 06.001-06.010. 06.003 to departmental stock as 97804.

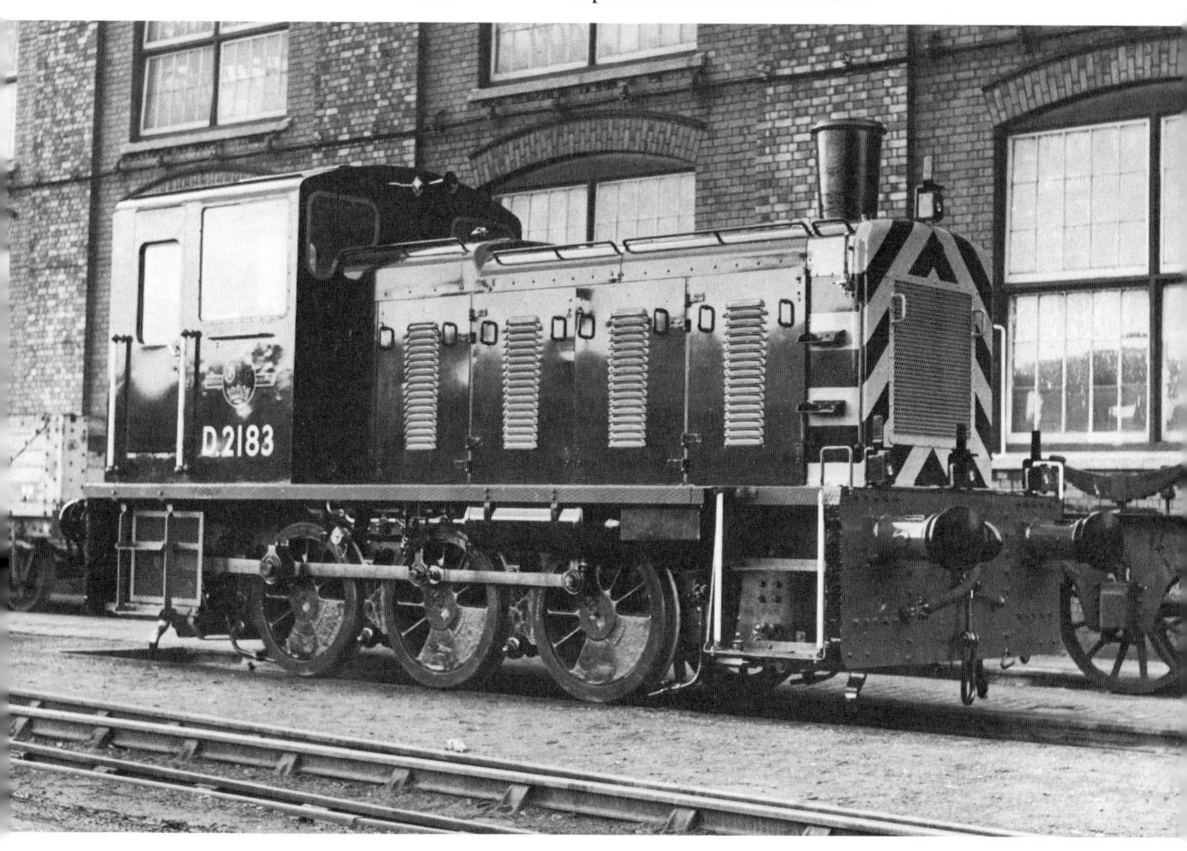

Below:
Used primarily on the Scottish Region, the Andrew Barclay 0-4-0 diesel-mechanical shunters which later became Class 06 were the last design of four coupled shunter to remain in service with BR. No D2433 is seen at Eastfield depot on 8 May 1966. *D. L. Percival*

Above:
Although a total of 69 members of the Hunslet 0-6-0DM design which was to become Class 05 were built, they were all withdrawn by BR by the late 1960s except for one which remained in use on the Isle of Wight until 1983. Here D2574 is seen in original condition on the Scottish Region.
BR Scottish Region

Class 07

Number series: D2985-D2998†
Engine: Paxman 6RPML MKIII
Cylinders: Six
Rating: 275hp at 1,360rpm
Transmission: One AEI axle-suspended traction motor
Maximum speed: 20mph

Wheel arrangement: 0-6-0DE
Driving wheel dia: 3ft 6in
Maximum TE: 28,240lb
Weight: 42ton
First loco built: June 1962
Last loco withdrawn: July 1977

† Later renumbered 07.001-07.013.

Built for use in Southampton Docks where they replaced the 'USA' 0-6-0T this class was a modern, attractive design with a good driver's view from the cab over the two low bonnets. A dramatic reduction in the traditional freight traffic to Southampton Docks rendered the class redundant and after a relatively short life the class was withdrawn, several being sold to industry.

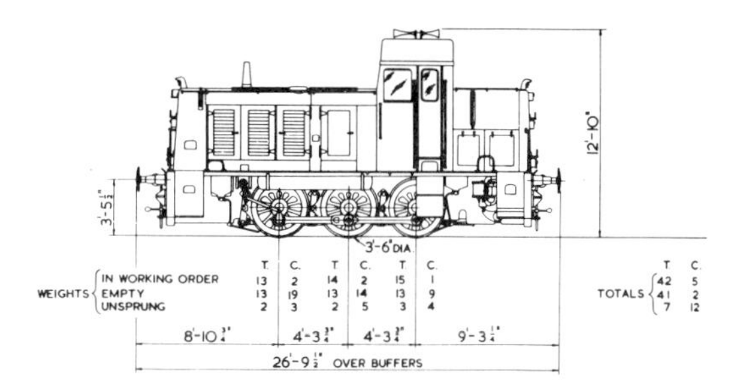

Above:
General arrangement of 275hp Class 07 diesel-electric 0-6-0.

Below:
Two members of Class 07 in final condition with BR blue livery and TOPS numbers. Nos 07.006 and 07.010 are seen at Southampton East depot on 30 June 1974. *B. J. Nicolle*

Classes 08, 09 and 10

Number series: D3000-D4192†
Engine: English Electric 6KT
Cylinders: Six
Rating: 350hp at 630rpm
Transmission: Two EE nose-suspended traction motors
Maximum speed: 20mph*

Wheel arrangement: 0-6-0DE
Driving wheel dia: 4ft 6in
Maximum TE: 35,000lb
Weight: 49ton
First loco built: October 1952

Note: details apply only to standard English Electric equipped Class 08. See accompanying table of variations.
* Class 09 maximum speed: 27mph
† D3000-D3366 originally numbered 13000-13366. Class later renumbered 08.001-08.958 and 09.001-09.026.

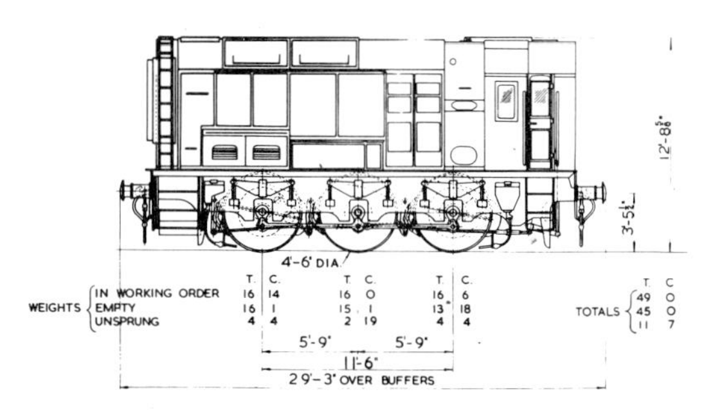

Left:
General arrangement of Standard 350hp Class 08 diesel-electric 0-6-0.

Above:
The standard BR diesel shunter, of which several hundred remain in service in the 1980s, dates back to the prewar LMS designs and has proved an eminently successful locomotive. Seen here in British Railways green livery is Class 08 No D3926.

With antecedents dating back to LMS developments in the 1930s, the standard BR diesel-electric shunters of Classes 08 and 09 are a veteran design. Replacement of steam shunting locomotives was an early preoccupation on the motive power side of the newly-formed British Railways, and the final version of the LMS 0-6-0 diesel shunter met the requirements almost unchanged. First orders for new locomotives were placed in 1952, with BR building the mechanical parts and English Electric supplying diesel engines and power equipment. Some structural changes were made so that the new series of shunters would be suitable for all Regions and yards. Wheel diameter was increased to 4ft 6in and tractive effort went up from 30,000lb to 35,000lb. The straight air brake operated two articulated brake blocks on one side of each wheel, while provision was made for controlling vacuum-braked stock. The changes increased the weight to 49 tons. They included provision for equipping the locomotives with other makes of diesel engine and transmission, but the first orders retained the English Electric 6KT naturally-aspirated (ie not turbo-charged) engine giving 350hp at 685rpm.

More manufacturers were involved in further orders placed in 1953, comprising 30 locomotives with Lister-Blackstone engines of 370hp at 750rpm and 10 with Crossley EST two-strokes giving 350hp at 825rpm. Fifteen of the Blackstone-engined locomotives had BTH electrical equipment, and the remainder were equipped by GEC (Class 10). The two-strokes had Crompton Parkinson equipment. The GEC/Blackstone combination was the only one to be repeated, 85 more of these power equipments being ordered. The locomotives with these three variations of the standard design were as follows:

Blackstone/BTH Nos D3152-66
Blackstone/GEC Nos D3137-51, D3439-53, D3473-502, D3612-51
Crossley/Crompton Parkinson Nos D3117-26

None of the above variants has survived and subsequent orders were for English Electric 6KT engines and electrical equipment. By mounting the belt-driven auxiliary generator and traction motor blower on a platform above the main machine the length of the engine-generator set is reduced, producing a compact locomotive. The generators are at the cab end, and the radiator at the forward end is close enough to the engine for the fan to be driven by a belt from a short crankshaft extension as in conventional automotive practice. Each outer coupled axle is driven through double-reduction gearing by a traction motor, the two machines being normally in parallel but with provision for off-load switching into series for hump shunting. Intermediate gears in the double-reduction gearcases can be removed so that the locomotive can be towed without the traction motors turning.

The driver's controller is linked mechanically to the engine governor and provides continuous control of engine speed after preliminary steps of generator field control. With the engine running at full speed, one step of field control resistance remains in circuit until the controller is moved to its final position, when it is cut out to give full power unless a heavy current demand has held the generator voltage below a preset figure, when the action is delayed. There is no automatic load regulator in these locomotives, the generator being designed with a natural characteristic which utilises full engine power over the small speed range involved. Class 08 locomotives are geared for a top speed of 20mph, and Class 09 for 27mph.

The most numerous modifications in the '08/09' fleet have been concerned with the change to air brakes. Many shunters now have a mechanical parking brake, direct air braking of their own wheels, additional compressor power for automatic air braking of vehicles, and provision for vacuum braked stock.

Class 11

Forerunner of standard BR 0-6-0 diesel electric shunter. Introduced by London, Midland & Scottish Railway, 1944. Equipped with English Electric 6KT engine. 106 examples absorbed by British Rail. Last locomotive withdrawn 1972. **Number series**: 12033-12138.

Class 12

Forerunner of standard BR 0-6-0 diesel electric shunter. Ordered by Southern Railway but first locomotive delivered from Ashford Works in April 1949. Equipped with English Electric 6KT engine. Fitted with Bulleid-Firth-Brown 'Boxpok' wheels. 26 examples built. Last locomotive withdrawn 1971. **Number series:** 15211-15236.

Class 13

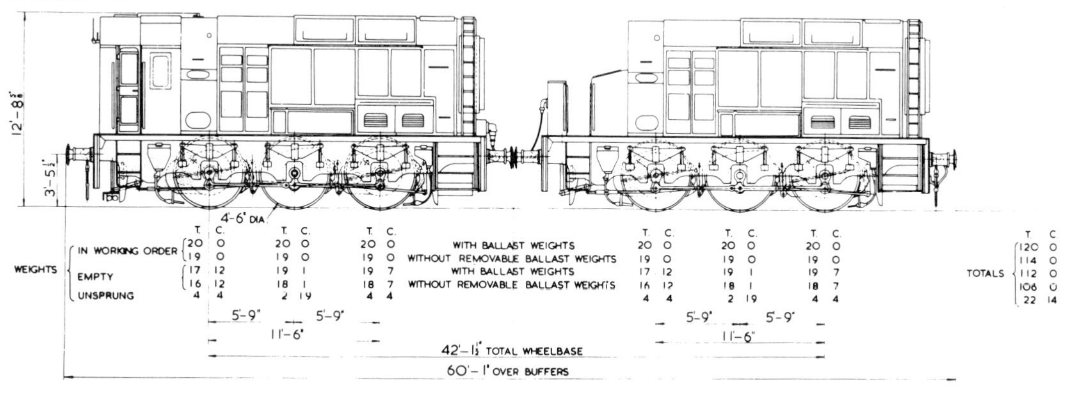

Above:
General arrangement of 700hp Class 13 diesel-electric 0-6-0+0-6-0.

In 1965 six '08' shunters were coupled in three pairs for shunting at Tinsley yard. The cab of one locomotive in each pair was removed and its power unit was controlled from the other cab, a pneumatic control replacing the direct mechanical linkage. These locomotives formed Class 13, which became extinct in early 1985 with the end of hump shunting at Tinsley.

Above:
Three Class 13 locomotives were built in the mid-1960s by coupling two Class 08 shunters, one with cab removed. Their purpose was hump shunting at Tinsley yard and No 13.003 is seen being refuelled at Tinsley depot on 18 August 1974. *B. J. Nicolle*

Class 15

Number series: D8200-D8243
Engine: Paxman 16YHXL
Cylinders: Sixteen, 7in × 7.75in
Rating: 800hp at 1,250rpm
Transmission: Four BTH nose-suspended traction motors
Maximum speed: 60mph
Wheel arrangement: Bo-Bo
Wheel dia: 3ft 3.5in
Continuous TE: 20,000lb at 10.5mph
Maximum TE: 37,500lb
Weight: 68ton
First loco built: November 1957
Last loco withdrawn: March 1971

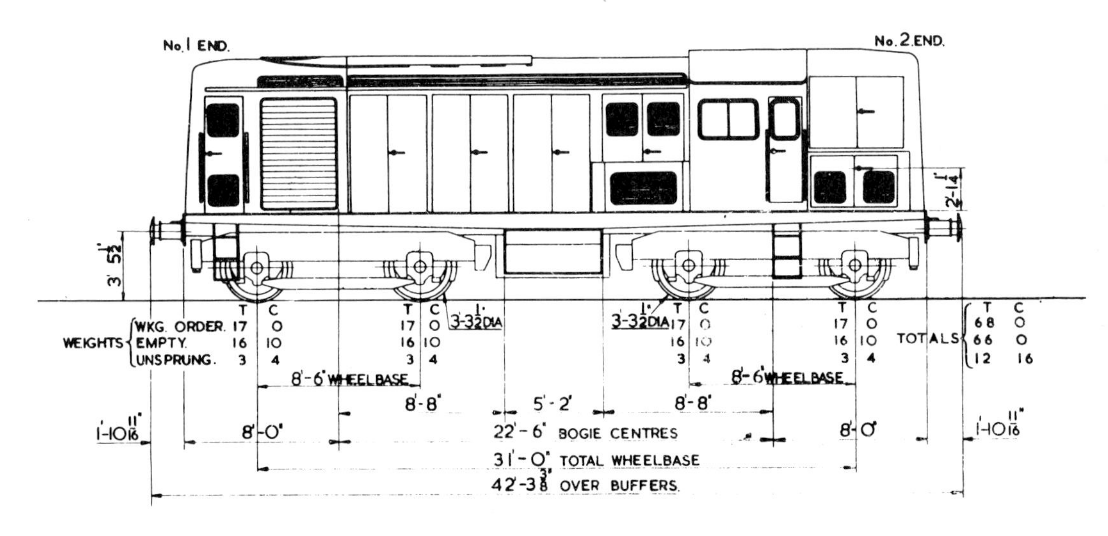

Above:
General arrangement of 800hp Class 15 diesel-electric Bo-Bo.

The second of the Type 1 locomotives ordered under the modernisation plan was an 800hp Bo-Bo designed by the British Thomson Houston Co Ltd (BTH), this company supplying the power equipment. Mechanical parts were built by the Clayton Equipment Co Ltd and the Yorkshire Engine Co Ltd, the latter undertaking final erection of the locomotives. The locomotive had a single cab with a long 'bonnet' type of casing over the power equipment, while a shorter compartment at the other end of the cab housed control equipment and certain auxiliaries. Radiator panels were side-mounted at the end of the bonnet remote from the cab, and air was drawn through them by a fan driven mechanically from the engine crankshaft through a gearbox. Pneumatic control of the governor provided infinitely variable engine speed. The main and auxiliary generators formed a single unit with the engine, with a separate belt-driven exciter.

Equalising beams were attached to the bottom faces of the bogie axleboxes and the coil spring primary suspension was damped by shock absorbers. Motor nose suspension was by vertical rubber-bushed links and a similar link between each motor and the bogie frame controlled lateral movement, reducing flange wear and improving riding. The four traction motors, driving through resilient gears, were connected in parallel and operated with one weak field step.

These locomotives were described officially as being for freight transfer and secondary passenger duties. Although not provided with train heating boilers, they had a through steam pipe so that steam could be supplied to rolling stock from a locomotive coupled ahead of them when working in multiple. After withdrawal, four of the class were modified for use as stationary train heating units.

Below:
One of the single cab BTH 800hp locomotives, later Class 15, No D8202 heads a typical freight train of the 1960s on the former GE main line to Cambridge on 23 August 1966.
P. H. Groom

Class 16

Number series: D8400-D8409
Engine: Paxman 16YHXL
Cylinders: Sixteen, 7in × 7.75in
Rating: 800hp at 1,250rpm
Transmission: Four GEC axle-hung, nose-suspended traction motors
Maximum speed: 60mph
Wheel arrangement: Bo-Bo
Wheel dia: 3ft 7in
Continuous TE: 20,000lb
Maximum TE: 42,000lb
Weight: 68ton
First loco built: May 1958
Last loco withdrawn: September 1968

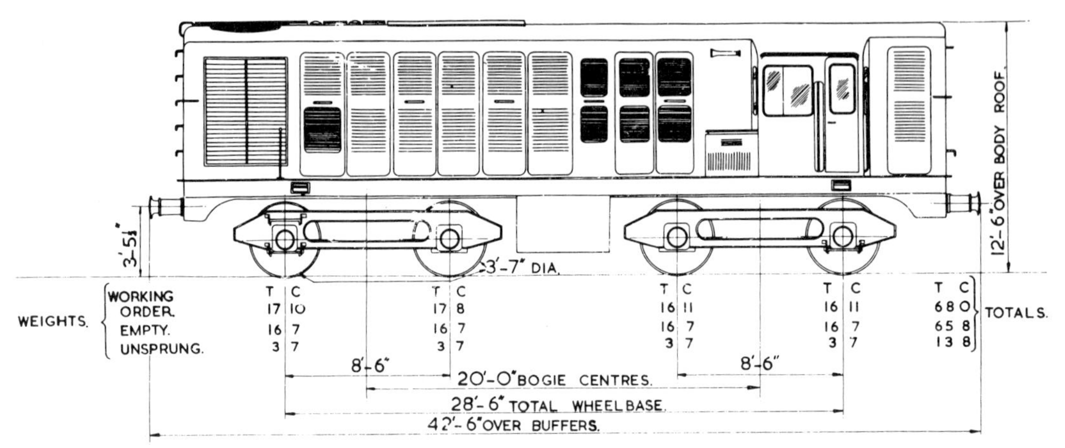

Above:
General arrangement of 800hp Class 16 diesel-electric Bo-Bo.

Below:
Another class of single cab Type 1 locomotives was built by NBL in 1958, later becoming Class 16. D8401 is seen at Stratford depot in May 1964. All members of this class were withdrawn during 1968 after a life of only 10 years.
P. H. Groom

A further 800hp Type 1 design came from GEC, working with the North British Locomotive Co Ltd as builder of the mechanical parts. This was again a single-cab locomotive with bonnet structure over the power equipment, and a smaller compartment at the rear of the cab for low-tension auxiliary switchgear and two motor-driven exhausters. The swing bolster bogies were of conventional design with two groups of coil springs and auxiliary rubber springs forming the secondary suspension. The control system comprised 10 notches, with two steps of excitation control by fixed resistances followed by eight engine speed control steps. Three weak-field steps could come into action from notch 3 onwards. At a predetermined value of current in the separately-excited field (ie the field controlled by the load regulator), a transition relay operated and a control relay was energised which caused the load regulator to reduce generator excitation and voltage until at a pre-set current the first weak-field contactors closed. A similar process brought in the two following steps if appropriate. Backward transition towards full field was also automatic, being initiated by a current relay in one motor circuit according to the load demanded from the generator.

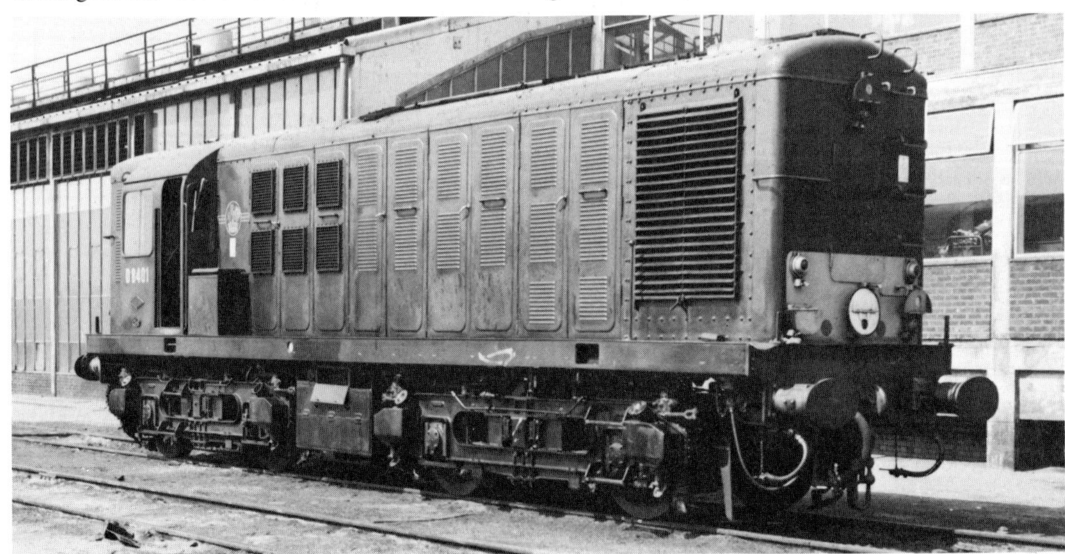

Class 17

Number series: D8500-D8616
Engines: Two, Paxman 6ZHXL*
Cylinders: Six
Rating: 450hp at 1,500rpm
Transmission: Four GEC axle-hung, nose-suspended traction motors
Maximum speed: 60mph

Wheel arrangement: Bo-Bo
Wheel dia: 3ft 3.5in
Continuous TE: 18,000lb at 13mph
Maximum TE: 40,000lb
Weight: 68ton
First loco built: September 1962
Last loco withdrawn: September 1971

Note: D8588-D8616 equipped with four Crompton Parkinson traction motors
*D8586/7 equipped with two Rolls-Royce eight-cyl. engines of 450hp.

Below:
General arrangement of 900hp Class 17 diesel-electric Bo-Bo.

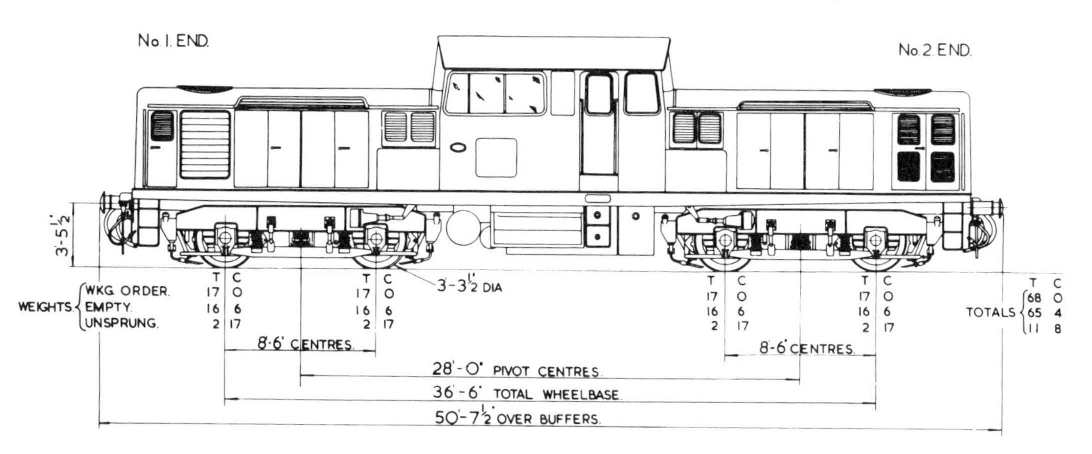

With a rating of 900hp from two diesel engines, Nos D8500-8616 were in the Type 1 power class. They differed from the other Type 1 designs in having a central cab, and in their high-speed (1,500rpm) engines. The view in both directions

Below:
The unconventional Clayton locomotives of Class 17 were also a somewhat short-lived design, although 117 of them were built, some being withdrawn after only five or six years in service. D8595 leaves Ryhope Grange sidings on 7 September 1967. *J. S. Hancock*

over the bonnets enclosing the power equipment was considerably better than from the cabs of the other classes because the horizontal engines allowed the bonnet height to be reduced compared with installations of vertical or vee engines. It had been decided to standardise centre cabs for future Class 1 locomotives because of the high proportion of shunting time in pick-up freight duties, but this policy was not implemented.

The first 88 locomotives were built by the Clayton Equipment Co Ltd. Provision was made for installing a train-heating boiler but was not put to use. The two bonnets were of equal length and each was in three sections: a radiator section, an engine compartment with a six-cylinder horizontal engine, and a generator compartment. The generator compartment was sealed off from the engine compartment to prevent the ingress of oil mist and dirt. Generator cooling air was discharged into the engine compartment so that it was slightly pressurised and an air flow to atmosphere through louvres in the compartment roof was established. Bogie design was conventional, with roller bearing axleboxes working in guides and linked by underslung equalising beams which fitted into stirrups cast integrally with the axleboxes. A dished centre pivot enabled the bogies to adjust themselves easily to the sharp reversal of gradient when working over humps in marshalling yards.

The first 88 locomotives had GEC electrical equipment with stepped control of engine speed and could not work in multiple with other classes. A traction selector switch enabled the locomotive to work with one engine shut down for fuel economy in shunting, when high tractive effort was required but speed was low. Other switch positions could be used to allow the locomotive to travel under its own power in the event of the failure of an engine, a generator or a traction motor. When troubles developed in the Paxman engines, two locomotives were equipped experimentally with Rolls-Royce engines, but when a second series of locomotives was ordered they were again fitted with Paxman engines. This batch of 29 was built by Beyer Peacock and had Crompton Parkinson electrical equipment. Continuous pneumatic control of engine speed replaced the earlier 'notched' system.

Class 20

Number series: D8000-D8327†
Engine: English Electric 8SVT Mk II
Cylinders: Eight, 10in × 12in
Rating: 1,000hp at 850rpm
Transmission: Four EE axle-hung, nose-suspended traction motors
Maximum speed: 75mph

Wheel arrangement: Bo-Bo
Wheel dia: 3ft 7in
Continuous TE: 19,500lb
Maximum TE: 42,000lb
Weight: 72ton
First loco built: June 1957

† Later renumbered 20.001-20.228

Below:
General arrangement of 1,000hp Class 20 diesel-electric Bo-Bo.

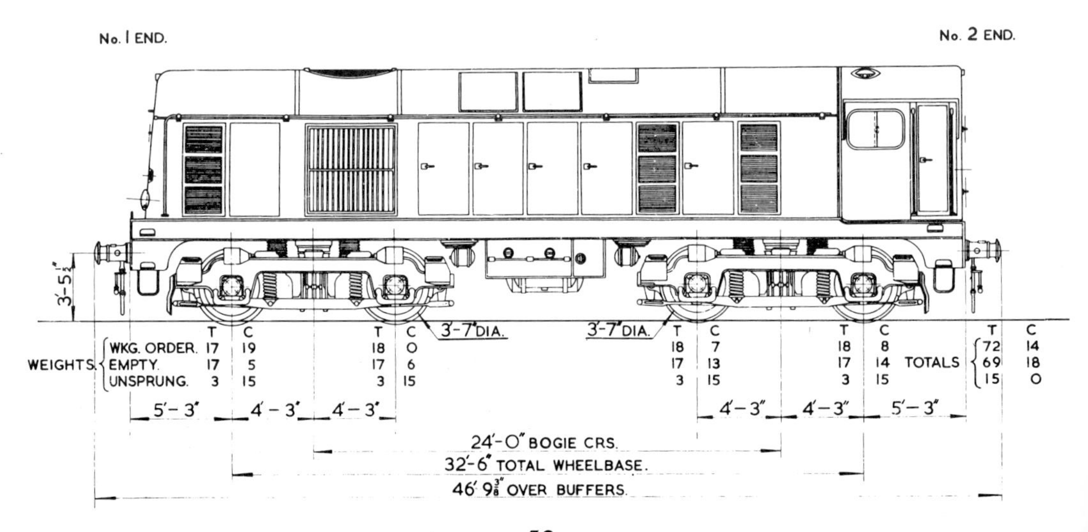

Locomotives of this 1,000hp Bo-Bo class were the first to be delivered of the 174 locomotives in four different power ranges ordered under the Modernisation Plan of 1955. Like others in the Type 1 power range (up to 1,000hp) they were a single cab design with the power equipment enclosed by a 'bonnet' structure, but the styling of the body as a whole was noticeably more elegant than in corresponding designs from other manufacturers. Class 20 was built entirely within the English Electric organisation. The engine was

Above:
One of the most successful diesel designs operated by BR has proved to be the English Electric Type 1 locomotives designated TOPS Class 20. D8002 heads another member of the class on a Broad Street-Carlisle freight. Both locomotives are in original green livery. *BR (LM)*

Below:
Later members of Class 20 were built with four character headcode panels, although these were no longer used after the mid-1970s. Nos 20.191 and 20.217, both in blue livery with yellow ends, are in charge of a rake of empty hopper wagons at Willington power station on 12 January 1984 – a typical Class 20 duty. *C. J. Tuffs*

the eight-cylinder 8SVT Mk II giving its rated output at 850rpm, and it formed a single power unit with the main and auxiliary generators. The generators were at the cab end of the locomotive. At the forward end of the engine the crankshaft was coupled to a mechanical drive to the radiator fan. Fuel tanks were contained within the underframe, which consisted of longitudinal girders plated over top and bottom, the centre portion being sealed to form a reservoir. Side doors on the bonnet structure gave access to the power equipment, and the roof sections over the control cubicle, power unit and end compartment were removable. Hinged hatches were provided over the cylinder heads and pressure chargers. The locomotive body was carried on each bogie by a single swing bolster supported from a spring plank by semi-elliptic springs. Primary suspension was by coil springs between equalising beams underslung from the axleboxes and the bogie frame. Originally roof access ladders were carried alongside the large radiator panels but they were later removed.

The cabs were equipped with two control desks, one for each direction of running. From analogy with steam practice, the cab used to be considered as being at the rear, the driver's view when travelling 'forwards' being along the bonnet. In practice the view was much better when travelling cab-first and this became the normal mode of operation. The locomotives can work in multiple and in recent years have generally been used in this way, working in pairs coupled bonnet to bonnet. Steam heating was not provided, but in summer pairs of Class 20s have done much work on summer seasonal trains between the Midlands and the East Coast. They are, of course, primarily a freight class, and a number were fitted with slow-speed control for working merry-go-round trains.

Classes 21 and 29

Number series: D6100-D6157*
Engine: NBL/MAN L12V18/21
Cylinders: Twelve, 7.1in × 8.3in
Rating: 1,100hp at 1,500rpm
Transmission: Four GEC nose-suspended traction motors
Maximum speed: 75mph
Wheel arrangement: Bo-Bo
Wheel dia: 3ft 7in
Continuous TE: 30,000lb at 10mph
Maximum TE: 45,000lb
Weight: 72ton 10cwt
First loco built: December 1958
Last loco withdrawn: August 1968

* Nos 6100-6109 rated at 1,000hp, continuous TE 25,000lb at 11mph.
Note: Twenty locomotives re-engined as Class 29

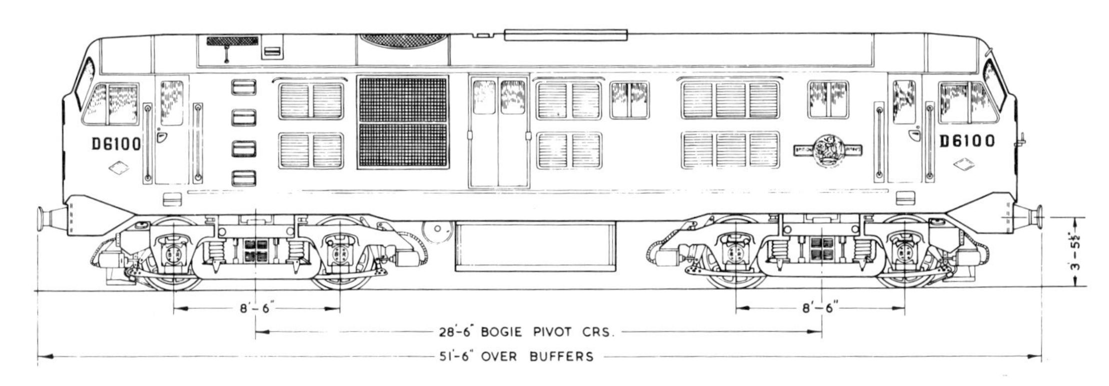

Below:
General arrangement of 1,100hp Class 21 diesel-electric Bo-Bo. *R. S. Carter*

Number series: Various ex Class 21
Engine: Paxman 12YJXL
Cylinders: Twelve
Rating: 1,350hp at 1,500rpm
Transmission: Four GEC nose-suspended traction motors
Maximum speed: 80mph
Wheel arrangement: Bo-Bo
Wheel dia: 3ft 7in
Continuous TE: 24,400lb at 16mph
Maximum TE: 47,000lb
Weight: 72ton 10cwt
First loco rebuilt: July 1963
Last loco withdrawn: December 1971

Above:
The first member of Class 21 to be fitted with a Paxman engine, thus becoming Class 29, was D6123 which is seen passing St Rollox with a Buchanan Street-Aberdeen train on 26 November 1963. The locomotive is in standard green livery with yellow warning panels. *N. Pollock*

These two classes of Type 2 Bo-Bo diesel-electric locomotive were basically similar but there were three engine variants. Ten had NBL/MAN engines set at 1,000hp, and the rest similar engines giving 1,100hp. Various engine problems arose and at a later stage 20 locomotives were re-equipped with Paxman Ventura engines of 1,350hp, being then reclassified as Class 29.

Electrical equipment was by GEC, who designed a main generator with a duplex lap winding to reduce flashover risks by maintaining a moderate voltage between the commutator segments. In the first locomotives with 1,000hp engines this machine had a continuous rating of 1,700A, 367V, with a maximum of 635V. In the 1,100hp locomotives the rating was increased to 1,940A, 367V, and 620V maximum. There were two forms of power control. Locomotives allocated originally to the Eastern Region had an electromagnetic stepped system with 10 notches, as follows: **1** fixed generator excitation with engine at idling speed; **2** generator excitation increased but engine speed unchanged; **3** generator excitation allowed to increase to maximum under control of load regulator; **4-10** engine speed and power increased in carefully regulated steps. The locomotives for the Scottish Region had pneumatic continuously variable control. All thc class was eventually transferred to the Scottish Region so as to be taken readily to the NBL works when needing attention.

The locomotives were carried on Commonwealth swing bolster bogies. A large-diameter bolster centre transmitted tractive and braking forces to the underframe through a boss engaging with it. There was no kingpin, but retaining brackets on the underframe engaged with the centre, allowing bogie and underframe to be lifted together and preventing excessive swivel of the bogie in case of derailment.

Above:
Members of Class 29 had their appearance significantly altered with the end gangway doors being removed and four character headcode panels fitted. Just over one year before final withdrawal 6130, still carrying green livery but with full yellow ends heads a football special over the Forth Bridge on 22 August 1970. *G. J. Jackson*

Class 23

Number series: D5900-D5909
Engine: Napier T9-29 Deltic
Cylinders: Nine
Rating: 1,100hp at 1,500rpm
Transmission: Four E E axle-hung, nose-suspended traction motors
Maximum speed: 75mph

Wheel arrangement: Bo-Bo
Wheel dia: 3ft 7in
Continuous TE: 31,800lb at 9mph
Maximum TE: 46,200lb
Weight: 73ton 17cwt
First loco built: April 1959
Last loco withdrawn: March 1971

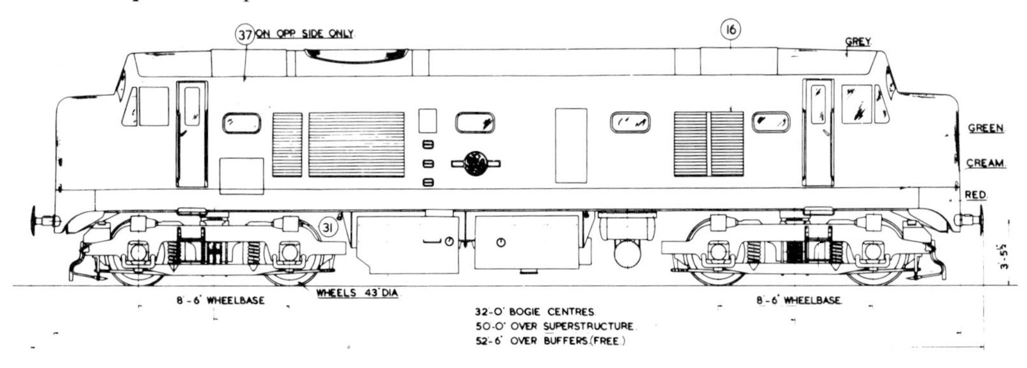

Above:
General arrangement of 1,100hp Class 23 diesel-electric Bo-Bo.

Under the 1955 modernisation plan the English Electric company received orders for locomotives in the three original power classifications, then known as Types A, B and C. Type B (later Type 2) covered the power range from 1,000 to 1,500hp and in this category English Electric supplied ten Bo-Bo locomotives with a nine-cylinder version of the 'Deltic' engine rated at 1,100hp at 1,600rpm. They were known unofficially as 'Baby Deltics'. A conventional in-line arrangement of the main and auxiliary generators was adopted, with one of the traction motor blowers coupled to the auxiliary generator shaft. At the other end of the engine the crankshaft was coupled to an auxiliary gearbox, from which drives were taken to the second traction motor blower, the air compressor and the radiator fan. A train heating boiler was installed behind one cab. Bogies were similar to those of the English Electric Class 20. 'Baby Deltics' worked mainly on outer suburban duties from King's Cross, going as far afield as the Cambridge line, and on empty stock duties.

The locomotives suffered from various problems associated with engine components and the auxiliary drive system. A proposal to re-engine them with a new vee-type English Electric engine then under development was dropped but the whole class underwent a thorough refurbishing. One of the measures taken was reduction of the load on the auxiliary gearbox by installing an electrically-driven compressor. A more evident change externally was removal of the gangway doors in the nose ends and the fitting of four-digit train-number indicators.

Refurbishing improved the reliability of the locomotives but after their return to service there was a crop of radiator troubles. In the meantime it had become BR traction policy to reduce the number of small, non-standard locomotive classes. Class 23 was in this category and its history to date had not been encouraging. Withdrawals began in September 1968. No D5901 outlived the others of its class by being transferred to Derby for work with the Railway Technical Centre, where it remained in use until 1975. It was finally cut up for scrap in 1977.

Below:
The 'Baby Deltic' Class 23 was built following the success of the original 'Deltic' design, but the smaller locomotives proved far from reliable in service. The brand new D5908 enters Kings Cross with a local train in May 1959.
M. S. Welch

Class 24

Number series: D5000-D5150†
Engine: Sulzer 6LDA28-A
Cylinders: Six, 11.02in × 14.17in
Rating: 1,160hp at 750rpm
Transmission: Four B.T.H. axle-hung, nose-suspended traction motors
Maximum speed: 90mph

Wheel arrangement: Bo-Bo
Wheel dia: 3ft 9in
Continuous TE: 21,300lb at 14.8mph
Maximum TE: 40,000lb
Weight: 75ton*
First loco built: July 1958
Last loco withdrawn: October 1980

* D5094-D5150 **weight**: 72ton 17cwt
† Later renumbered 24.001-24.150

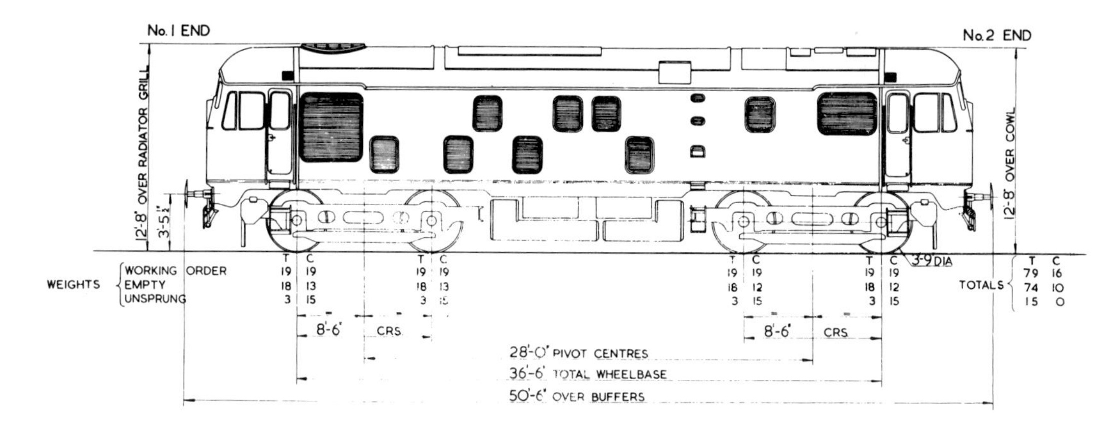

Above:
General arrangement of 1,160hp Class 24 diesel-electric Bo-Bo.

To describe a face as 'homely' is something less than a compliment, but the word comes to mind in looking at pictures of British Rail's locomotive design for the 1,001-1,500hp (Type 2) power class. In spite of this, a long life of hard work and dispersal all over the BR system on a wide range of passenger and freight duties earned high regard for these Class 24 diesel-electric locomotives, and their passing was mourned.

The first 20 locomotives of Class 24 were built at Derby. As the class multiplied, orders went to the BR works at Crewe and Darlington. Class 24 was a mixed traffic Bo-Bo powered by a Sulzer 6LDA28-A six-cylinder in-line engine of 1,160hp. The electrical transmission equipment was supplied by the British Thomson-Houston Co Ltd (BTH). In the body construction the underframe, the framework supporting the bodyside panels, and the cross-bracing at the top, formed an integral unit. There was a clue to this form of construction in the air filter apertures in the bodysides, which were spaced to be clear of the frame members. The swing-bolster bogies had outside frames, behind which were the axlebox guides and underslung equalising beams. The radiators and motor-driven fan were behind one end cab, and the train-heating boiler behind the other, the central portion of the body being occupied by the engine-generator set. In early locomotives of the class (later classified '24/0') excitation for the main generator came from a separate belt-driven exciter. In further construction changes were made to reduce the locomotive weight, and the exciter was dispensed with, excitation being taken from the auxiliary generator. These locomotives were classified '24/1'. They began with No D5050 and included 10 for freight duties only, without steam-heating boilers or water tanks. The power circuit consisted of four traction motors in parallel. Three weak-field steps were provided by diverter resistances. The weak-field contactors were operated by a motor-driven camshaft.

The locomotives were equipped at first with disc headcodes. When the four-digit descriptions were introduced, later locomotives were built with head code panels at roof level.

Below:
The BR-built Class 24 was first ordered under the 1955 Modernisation Plan and the Sulzer power unit used in it was to be the basis of a large fleet of Type 2 locomotives. D5010 stands at Ashford with a Maidstone East-Margate train on 19 September 1959. *D. C. Ovenden*

Class 25

Number series: D5151-D5299, D7500-D7677†
Engine: Sulzer 6LDA28-B
Cylinders: Six, 11.02in × 14.17in
Rating: 1,250hp at 750rpm
Transmission: Four AEI nose-suspended traction motors
Maximum speed: 90mph

Wheel arrangement: Bo-Bo
Wheel dia: 3ft 9in
Continuous TE: 20,800lb
Maximum TE: 45,000lb*
Weight: Various 70ton 5cwt-74ton 8cwt
First loco built: April 1961
Last loco withdrawn:

* D5151-D5175 **Maximum TE**: 39,000lb
† Later renumbered 25.001-25.327

Below:
General arrangement of 1,250hp Class 25/0 diesel-electric Bo-Bo.

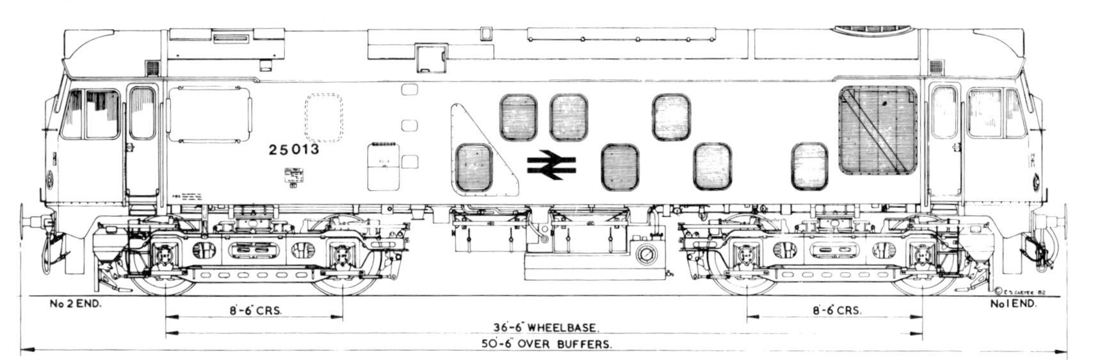

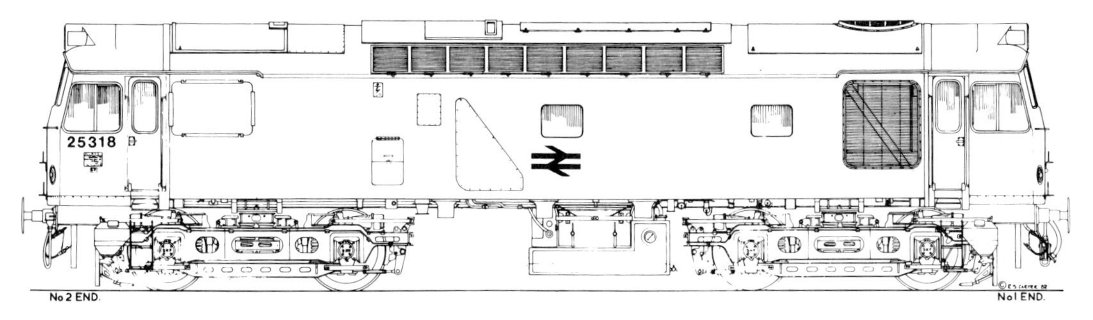

Above:
General arrangement of 1,250hp Class 25/3 diesel-electric Bo-Bo. *R. S. Carter*

As withdrawals of steam locomotives accelerated, the requirement for Type 2 diesels increased. By 1959 Sulzer could offer an uprated version of its six-cylinder engine, the 1,250hp output being given at the same speed of 750rpm as in the earlier type. The new engine was intercooled and incorporated other improvements, and was designated 6LDA28-B. This was the engine chosen for the next batch of Type 2 locomotives built by BR. They formed Class 25 under the 1973 classification.

Construction of Class 25 was shared between Derby and Darlington but 36 were built by Beyer Peacock at Gorton to relieve pressure on BR works. The first locomotives began to enter service in 1961. By that time BTH, the supplier of electrical equipment for Class 24, had become part of the Associated Electrical Industries Group. At first the same types of generators and traction motors were used but worked at higher ratings. Gear ratio was altered, however, to allow a top speed of 90mph. These changes applied to the first 25 locomotives which subsequently became Class 25/0.

With the altered gear ratio, tractive effort was reduced compared with Class 24. The next batch were equipped with new traction motors and differently rated main generators, restoring the tractive effort at starting to the Class 24 figure. The new equipment made it necessary to change the motor grouping from four motors in parallel to two series pairs in parallel, while to extend the speed range over which full engine power could be used,

Above:
The wide-ranging Class 25, built by BR at Derby and Darlington was a development of Class 24. In green livery with yellow warning panels, D5203 and D5207 working in multiple approach Elstree New Tunnel with an up freight on 12 October 1963. *B. Stephenson*

Left:
The final development of the BR Type 2, Class 25/3 differed externally in a cleaner body design, without end gangways. In blue livery with full yellow ends, 25.283 approaches Gresty Lane No 1 signal box with a Crewe-Cardiff service on 26 May 1978. *B. J. Nicolle*

the number of weak-field steps was increased from three to six. These locomotives became Classes 25/1 and 25/2, there being some minor equipment differences between the two series. Both had a new design of driver's control pedestal and instrument display; in Class 25/0 these items had been similar to Class 24. With Class 25/2 there was a change in body design, the filters being removed from the bodysides to cantrail level, but 30 of this class had '25/1' bodyshells.

The third sub-division of Class 25 resulted from the installation of a redesigned generator which slightly reduced starting tractive effort but extended the speed range over which full engine power could be used. These locomotives began coming out in 1966, by which time various technical improvements had taken place and electronics were beginning to find a place in locomotive engineering. One of the results was that field-weakening was initiated at set speeds by electronic processing of the signals from a tachometer.

Class 26

Number series: D5300-D5346†
Engine: Sulzer 6LDA28-A
Cylinders: Six, 11.02in × 14.17in
Rating: 1,160hp at 750rpm
Transmission: Four Crompton Parkinson axle-hung, nose-suspended traction motors
Maximum speed: 90mph

Wheel arrangement: Bo-Bo
Wheel dia: 3ft 7in
Continuous TE: 30,000lb
Maximum TE: 40,000lb
Weight: 73ton 6cwt*
First loco built: July 1958

* D5300-D5319 **weight**: 77ton 17cwt
† Later renumbered 26.001-26.046

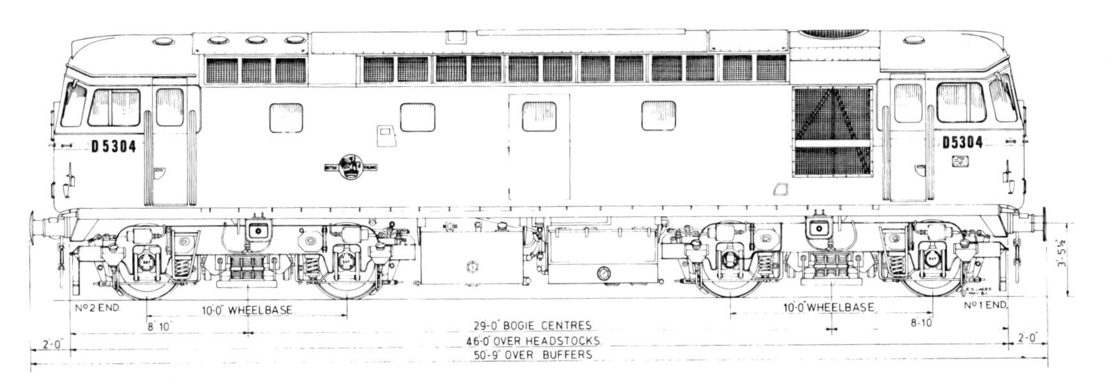

Top:
General arrangement of 1,160hp Class 26 diesel-electric Bo-Bo. *R. S. Carter*

Above:
BRCW built a Type 2 design equipped with the same Sulzer power unit as Class 24 built by BR. Two members of Class 26, Nos D5300 and D5309 power an Edinburgh-Aberdeen express past Camperdown Junction in April 1961.
T. Mahoney

At the same time as ordering the first 20 Type 2 locomotives from its own works, BR placed a contract for 20 more to a similar specification with the Birmingham Railway Carriage & Wagon Co Ltd (BRCW). They had the same Sulzer 1,160hp engine and common constructional features but by some alchemy which is hard to define, the body styling of the BRCW locomotives gave them a more energetic look. It seemed to stem from the end contours, emphasised by the cream colour of the cab upper panels and the similar lining on the bodysides. The placing of the air filter panels at cantrail level gave a neater appearance than the apparently haphazard arrangement of the corresponding panels in the early '24s', and a row of four windows in the bodysides, one of them in a side access door, complemented the row of filters above.

Electrical equipment was supplied by Crompton Parkinson Ltd. Excitation for the main generator was taken from the auxiliary machine in all these locomotives. The four traction motors were connected in parallel and drove through resilient gears with a ratio designed for a top speed of 80mph, 5mph higher than in Class 24. Field-weakening was in five steps and operated by a motor-driven camshaft. Another 26 locomotives of the class were built, but were equipped with lighter traction motors and incorporated other weight-saving features. The earlier locomotives were classified '26/0' in the BR renumbering, the remainder being '26/1'. Seven '26/0' locomotives were fitted for merry-go-round working in Scotland in 1966, a change which involved removing the train-heating boiler and incidentally reduced weight to a figure closer to that of the locomot with lighter traction motors.

The first 20 Class 26 locomotives went originally to the Eastern Region for suburban and certain semi-fast workings from Kings Cross. In 1960 the whole class was transferred to Scotland, where on internal services of all kinds they became a characteristic of the railway scene until their territory began to be eroded by Class 37 Co-Cos in the 1980s.

Bogies were a swing bolster type similar in principle to those of the BR Class 24s but the equalising beams were within the box section bogie side frames and rested on the axleboxes. Primary suspension was by coil springs carried by hangers from the beams, and secondary suspension by laminated springs. Traction and braking forces were transmitted by manganese steel links on the bolster and bogie while the centre pivot took the load through hard bronze liners on the top and bottom bearing faces.

Class 27

Number series: D5347-D5415†
Engine: Sulzer 6LDA28-B
Cylinders: Six, 11.02in × 14.17in
Rating: 1,250hp at 750rpm
Transmission: Four GEC axle-hung, nose-suspended traction motors
Maximum speed: 90mph

Wheel arrangement: Bo-Bo
Wheel dia: 3ft 7in
Continuous TE: 25,000lb
Maximum TE: 40,000lb
Weight: 72ton 10cwt
First loco built: June 1961

† Later renumbered 27.001-27.044, 27.101-27.112 and 27.201-27.212, Later 27.001-27.066

Below:
General arrangement of 1,250hp Class 27 diesel-electric Bo-Bo. *R. S. Carter*

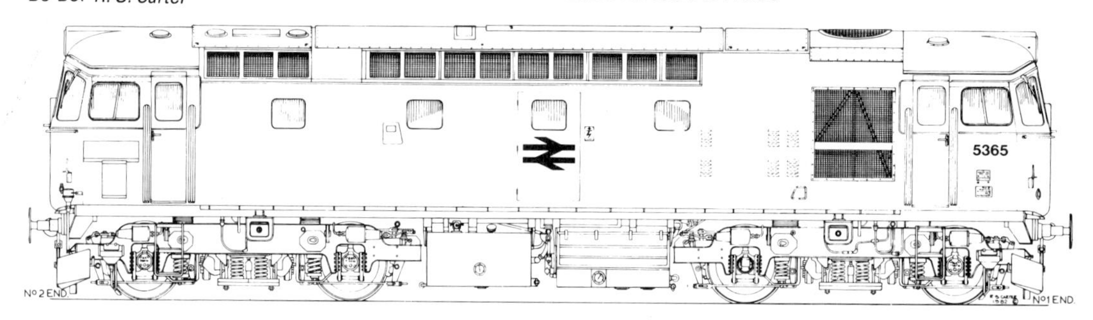

A further series of BRCW Type 2 locomotives was built with the Sulzer 1,250hp 6LDA28-B engine and became Class 27. Electrical equipment for this series was supplied by GEC. The power circuit took the usual form of four traction motors in parallel across a main generator with excitation from the 110V auxiliary system. Field-weakening, in three steps, was controlled by individual electro-pneumatic contactors instead of by camshaft as in Classes 24, 25 and 26. Class 27 was first distributed between the Scottish, North Eastern and London Midland Regions but in the late 1960s most were concentrated in Scotland. Here the locomotives came into the limelight when they were called upon to take over an accelerated express service between Edinburgh and Glasgow. On this duty they worked

Above:
From D5347 onwards the BRCW Type 2 locomotives were fitted with the uprated Sulzer engine and became Class 27. The most obvious external difference was the four character headcode panel above the cab windows, as seen on D5379 during driver training on the Bedford-Northampton line when new. *A. Swain*

in pairs, one at the front and one at the rear of six-coach sets of Mk II stock, the pneumatic control system being extended through the train to set the governor on the locomotive under remote control. Class 27 was geared for 90mph maximum speed and on these push-pull services the locomotives had to run continuously at close to the maximum for considerable distances. When electric heating was installed in the trains, the power supply was taken from a 120kW diesel-alternator set installed in the locomotives in place of the steam-heating boiler so as not to increase the load on the traction generator. The 24 locomotives converted for these services were classified '27/1' if push-pull but retaining steam heating, and '27/2' if push-pull with electric heating.

Nine locomotives were built without train-heating boilers for freight work from Thornaby, working mostly in pairs. In 1965 they were transferred to Leicester, but went with the others of the class to the Scottish Region in 1968-70. When Class 47 locomotives took over the Edinburgh-Glasgow push-pull workings, the Class 27s which had been modified for those duties had their special equipment removed during the period 1982-84 and reverted to basic Class 27s ('27/0').

Some mechanical changes were made in the design compared with Class 26. Coil springs replaced elliptical in the secondary suspension and shock absorbers were fitted to restrain lateral movements of the bogie bolster. The locomotives were built as new with roof-mounted four-digit description panels at roof level, the horns being removed to the buffer beams.

Class 28

Number series: D5700-D5719
Engine: Crossley HST V8
Cylinders: Eight
Rating: 1,200hp at 625rpm
Transmission: Five Metropolitan-Vickers axle-hung, nose-suspended traction motors
Maximum speed: 75mph
Wheel arrangement: Co-Bo
Wheel dia: 3ft 3.5in
Continuous TE: 25,000lb
Maximum TE: 50,000lb
Weight: 97ton
First loco built: October 1958
Last loco withdrawn: December 1968

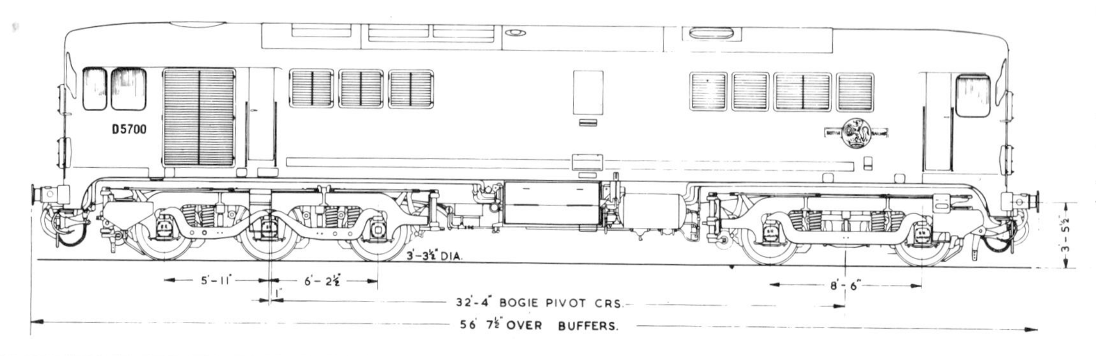

Top:
General arrangement of 1,200hp Class 28 diesel-electric Co-Bo.

Above:
The most obvious feature of the Metro-Vick Class 28 design was the odd combination of four and six wheel bogies, but the two-stroke Crossley engine was equally unusual. D5715 passes Carnforth No 1 Junction signalbox with a Workington-Manchester service on 15 August 1964.
D. Cross

Two-stroke diesels for rail traction were widely used in the United States but in Great Britain the only examples in main line service were the opposed-piston engines in the 'Deltics' and the conventional two-strokes in Class 28. This class, built by Metropolitan-Vickers/Beyer, Peacock, is better known for its unusual Co-Bo wheel arrangement than for its power plant.

The two-stroke engine develops a more regular torque than the four-stroke, having one power stroke per revolution, but it is more difficult to secure complete evacuation of the burned gases. There is greater liability to carbon deposits and overheating of pistons, while the scope for supercharging is more limited than in the four-stroke. Against these difficulties is the fact that the engine has no mechanical valve gear, inlet and exhaust being controlled by the movement of the piston past ports in the cylinder walls. The Class 28 engine worked on the loop scavenge system in which the incoming air is directed towards the cylinder head and then curves down towards the exhaust port, pushing the burnt gases ahead of it. Pressure charging was enhanced by the Crossley exhaust pulse principle. Scavenge air which entered the exhaust manifold was forced back by the exhaust pressure pulse from an adjacent cylinder. By this means a positive pressure of about 10lb/sq in was created at the beginning of compression.

The five powered axles of the Co-Bo design gave the locomotive the high starting tractive effort of 50,000lb within an acceptable weight. Both bogies had equalising beams between the axles, their ends supported on top of the axleboxes by bonded rubber sandwiches. Shock absorbers were installed between the body and the bogie frames, and in parallel with the coil springs carrying the bolster. The diesel engine and generators were positioned at the six-wheel bogie end of the locomotive. An unusual feature of the assembly was that the main compressor was flange-mounted to the auxiliary generator and driven from it. There were three motor blowers, two for traction motor cooling and one to pressurise the generator compartment for forced cooling of the generator.

Power was controlled by a handwheel with ten positions. On 1 and 2 the engine idled but generator excitation was increased. On the other eight notches engine speed was increased in steps. Field-weakening was controlled direct by the load regulator, without separate contactors. There were two weak-field running steps, but each was approached through intermediate steps to avoid an abrupt change of field strength.

Today the Co-Bos are most often associated with their early work in pairs on the 'Condor' express container service between Hendon and Glasgow, forerunner of the Freightliner trains of later years. While on the LMR they also made a few appearances on St Pancras-Manchester expresses but those who went forth to see them so employed were often disappointed by failures to appear. For a time they brought a little novelty to the daily journey to the City from the Midland suburbs by working through trains to and from Moorgate. Then the London area knew them no more, but in due course it was reported that after a period of retreat due to engine failures they had returned to normal life on the old Furness Railway lines. It was only a respite; withdrawals into store began in 1965 and by 1968 the whole class had gone except for one which was retained for departmental work with the Research Department, and later for use as a train-heating unit. This survivor has been reconditioned and preserved.

Classes 30 and 31

Number series: D5500-D5517, D5519*
Engine: Mirrlees JVS12T*
Cylinders: Twelve, 9.75in × 10.5in
Rating: 1,250hp at 850rpm
Transmission: Four Brush nose-suspended traction motors
Maximum speed: 80mph

Wheel arrangement: AIA-AIA
Driving wheel dia: 3ft 7in
Continuous TE: 22,400lb at 16.5mph
Maximum TE: 42,000lb
Weight: 104ton
First loco built: October 1957
Last loco withdrawn: October 1980

* All rebuilt with English Electric 12SVT twelve-cylinder engine rated at 1,470hp.
† Later renumbered 31.001-31.019

Below:
General arrangement of 1,365 or 1,470hp Class 31 diesel-electric A1A-A1A.

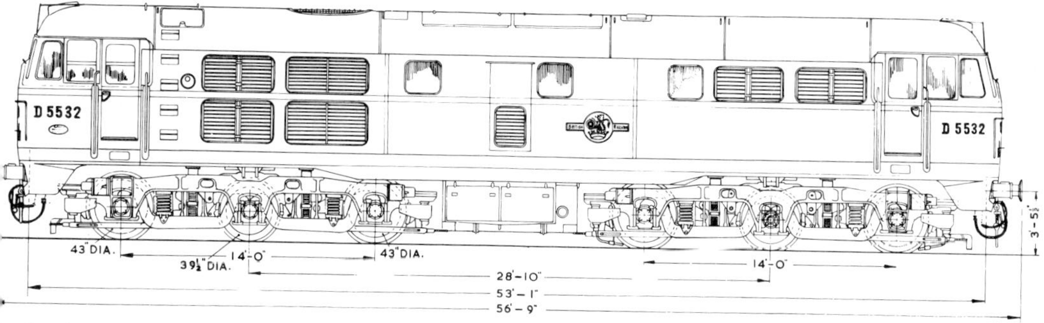

n the days of heavy, slow-running diesel engines, xle-loads had to be carefully watched and the esigners of the 1,250hp Brush Type 2 locomotive pread its 104 tons over six axles. In each three-axle ogie the two outer axles were motored, while the entre axle was simply a weight-carrier and had heels of smaller diameter. Main contractor for the locomotives was the Brush Electrical Engineering Co Ltd of Loughborough (now Brush Electrical Machines Ltd and a member of the Hawker-Siddeley Group). Construction of the underframes and bogies was shared between Beyer, Peacock & Co Ltd and W. G. Bagnall Ltd.

The superstructure was built in sections

Number series: D5518-D5520, D5862†
Engine: Mirrlees JVS12T*
Cylinders: Twelve, 9.75in × 10.5in
Rating: 1,365hp at 900rpm
Transmission: Four Brush nose-suspended traction motors
Maximum speed: 90mph
Wheel arrangement: AIA-AIA
Driving wheel dia: 3ft 7in
Continuous TE: 22,400lb at 16.5mph
Maximum TE: 42,000lb
Weight: 104ton
First loco built: October 1958

* D5545, D5655-D5670 engines uprated to 1,600hp at 950rpm. D5835 temporarily equipped with Mirrlees engine rated 2,000hp.
Entire class rebuilt from 1964 with English Electric 12SVT twelve-cylinder engine rated 1,470hp.
† Later renumbered 31.101-31.468

Below:
No D5500, the first member of Class 30 (later 31/0) is seen as delivered new to British Railways in October 1957. The locomotive is fitted with train identification discs instead of the later standard heacode panels. *P. F. Winding/IAL*

comprising two cab ends, four removable roof sections, and six removable side panels, two of which extended for the length of the diesel engine on each side of the body. Hatches in the roof gave access to the cylinder heads without the roof having to be removed. The body was carried on Commonwealth swing bolster bogies, the bolsters supported from the spring planks by elliptical springs. Equalising beams between the outer and inner axles curved upwards at the ends to rest on top of the axleboxes, the lower portion between the axles forming a platform for the coil springs of the primary suspension.

The 12-cylinder vee engine was the Mirrlees JVS12T set to give 1,250hp at 850rpm and was a modified version of the engine which powered 25 locomotives supplied earlier by Brush to the Ceylon Government Railway. The engine in the Ceylon locomotives was, in fact, the first rail traction diesel from the old-established firm of Mirrlees, Bickerton & Day. In the first 20 locomotives, engine speed and power were controlled in steps by an electromagnetic system. Three solenoids acted on a triangular plate linked with the governor. By energising the solenoids in various combinations, the compression of the spring was varied to provide several operating speeds. A fourth solenoid started and stopped the engine. These locomotives became Class 31/0 and could only operate in multiple with each other or with locomotives having a similar 'stepped' control system. In all later batches this form of control was replaced by a straight pneumatic system providing continuous variation of governor loading by means of a self-lapping air valve in the driver's controller.

In the next two batches of locomotives the engine was uprated to 1,365hp, now running at 900rpm. In a further boost of power the engines in a number of locomotives were equipped with oil-cooled pistons and speeded to 950rpm and 1,600hp. These ratings were lowered to the original 1,250hp after trouble began to be experienced with crankcases. Problems with traction diesels were not unusual at this time when diesel engineers were adapting their products to the locomotive environment just as electronic engineers would have to do in a few years time, but the reputation of the Brush Type 2s was unfairly sullied by a failure occurring at a most inopportune moment and receiving maximum publicity. On January 1961 No D5667 broke down south o

Cambridge while hauling a train in which the Queen was travelling. The locomotive was brand new and accompanied by two Brush fitters as a precaution against just such a mishap. But all to no avail, and a steam locomotive had to be summoned, with a delay of nearly an hour before the journey was resumed.

Crankcase failures reached a peak in 1963 and BR decided to re-engine the whole class with English Electric engines similar to those in Class 37, but derated to 1,470hp. Locomotives with EE engines were Class 31 and those with Mirrlees engines Class 30.

While still powered by axle-hung motors, the class reflected the trends of the time in having resilient gears and nose suspension with rubber-bushed attachment to the bogie transom and the motor frame. After the first batch of 20 locomotives, subsequent builds had modified traction motors allowing a top speed of 90mph. Train-heating boilers have been removed from many locomotives now confined to freight work. Those with regular passenger turns have been modified for electric train heating by replacing the original dc auxiliary generator with an alternator. They form Class 31/4.

Above:
Most members of Class 31 were built with headcode panels above the cabs as seen in this view of No 5668 hauling a well loaded ballast train at Peterborough on 30 July 1970. The locomotive is still in green livery with full yellow ends, whilst No 5596 in the background is carrying an early version of BR blue livery. *J. H. Cooper-Smith*

Class 33

Number series: D6500-D6597†
Engine: Sulzer 8LDA28-A
Cylinders: Eight, 11.02in × 14.17in
Rating: 1,550hp at 750rpm
Transmission: Four Crompton Parkinson axle-hung, nose-suspended traction motors
Maximum speed: 85mph

Wheel arrangement: Bo-Bo
Wheel dia: 3ft 7in
Continuous TE: 26,000lb at 17.5mph
Maximum TE: 45,000lb
Weight: 73ton 8cwt*
First loco built: December 1959

* Class 33/1 **weight:** 77ton 6cwt:
Class 33/2 **weight:** 74ton 4cwt.
† Later renumbered 33.001-33.065, 33.101-33.119 and 33.201-33.212

Below:
General arrangement of 1,550hp Class 33/0 diesel-electric Bo-Bo.

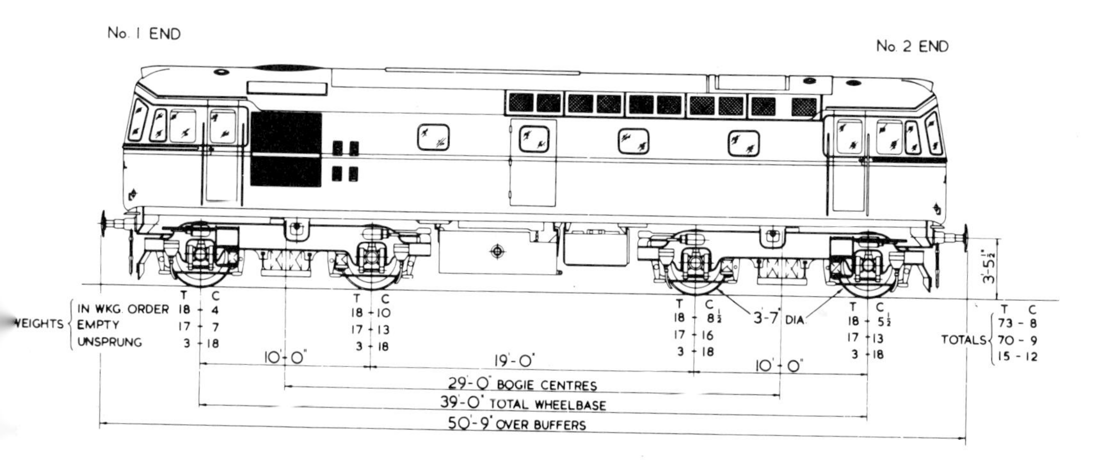

While moving towards EMU operation of all its main line services, the Southern Region had to provide for other types of passenger train and freight workings. Electric locomotives went part of the way, but the electric locomotives were confined to the live rail, and the ideal of electro-diesels of equal power in both modes of working had not been realised. A specification was therefore drawn up for a 'straight' diesel locomotive for freight and passenger work with a reserve of power for electric train heating. There was to be no steam boiler, the Southern's own stock being electrically heated, while inter-regional trains could be formed of stock with dual-heating. The various specification requirements were met within acceptable weight and cost limits by a Bo-Bo locomotive which was virtually a BRCW Type 2 with a 1,550hp engine, putting it in the Type 3 category.

The Southern Region Type 3 (or Class 33) locomotive is powered by a Sulzer 8LDA28 engine, an eight-cylinder version of the intercooled 6LDA28-A. Both are in-line engines running at 750rpm. The generator group, direct-coupled to the engine, consists of train-heating, main traction and auxiliary armatures on the same shaft. To conform with the two-pole heating circuit of BR ETH stock, the heating generator is a dc machine. Later conversions of other classes for ETH have used alternators, but the ac is rectified. When heating is in use the engine idles at 550rpm instead of the normal 350rpm with the controller 'off'. On moving the controller to start the train, the engine speed falls towards the normal idling condition and heating is briefly interrupted. It is resumed when the controller has been moved nearly half its travel and the engine has been accelerated correspondingly.

Electrical equipment was supplied by Crompton Parkinson as for Class 26, but the main generator and motors are more highly rated although of similar dimensions. Five steps of field-weakening are provided by individual diverter resistances in parallel, each with its own contactor, in place of the tapped resistance and three contactors in Class 26.

Engine speed is continuously variable by the usual pneumatic system. Locomotives modified for push-pull working between Bournemouth and Weymouth (Class 33/1) are equipped so that when under remote control from a driving trailer, four engine speeds are selected by an electro-pneumatic relay. These correspond to the four positions of the standard four-position EMU controller. Push-pull

Below:
Similar in appearance to Class 26, the Southern Region's BRCW Class 33s are powered by a larger Sulzer engine putting them in the Type 3 category. Green liveried D6573 heads a Fawley bound oil tank train between Millbrook and Redbridge on 5 January 1967. *J. H. Bird*

Above right:
One of the Class 33/1 locomotives fitted for push-pull operation with MU stock, D6536 is pictured between Bournemouth and Branksome with the Weymouth portion of a down Waterloo service, consisting of a 4TC set in original blue livery. *BR Southern Region*

operation has also been extended to Waterloo-Salisbury services. A Class 33 can control the motors of an EMU in the formation of its train. One working of this kind has been on a service from Waterloo to Eastleigh and Salisbury, dividing at Basingstoke, the Class 33 proceeding to Salisbury with four trailers and the EMU portion at the rear continuing under its own power to Eastleigh.

Mechanical construction was generally similar to that of the BRCW Type 2s but nose end doors were omitted, and secondary suspension was with coil springs. The standard Southern two-character headcode was displayed in the centre panel of the cab front. Twelve locomotives ('33/2') were built with flat bodysides to reduce the width so that they could work between Tunbridge Wells and Hastings, where tunnels restrict the loading gauge. All locomotives were equipped with the automatic air brakc, with provision for controlling vacuum brakes on a train from the same handle. This was in contrast with contemporary practice of a straight air brake on the locomotive controlled by the driver's vacuum brake handle, but was a logical arrangement for the Southern whose passenger stock was air-braked. One of the specification requirements for Class 33 was that it should be able to haul trains of EMU stock at normal service speeds in the event of a widespread power failure.

Class 37

Number series: D6600-D6608, D6700-D6999†
Engine: English Electric 12CSVT
Cylinders: Twelve, 10in × 12in
Rating: 1,750hp at 850rpm
Transmission: Six E.E. axle-hung, nose-suspended traction motors
Maximum speed: 90mph
Wheel arrangement: Co-Co
Wheel dia: 3ft 7in
Continuous TE: 35,000lb at 13.6mph
Maximum TE: 55,500lb
Weight: 100ton-105ton
First loco built: December 1960

† Later renumbered 37.001-37.308
Also from 1985, 37.401-37.431

Below:
General arrangement of 1,750hp Class 37 diesel-electric Co-Co. *R. S. Carter*

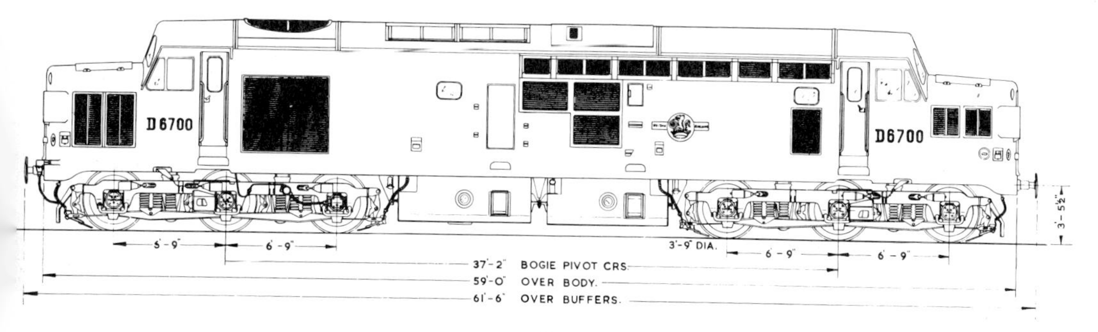

The Southern's diesel-electric locomotive was in the middle of the Type 3 power range. At the time of its introduction, the English Electric SVT range of diesel engines was being further developed by intercooling, achieving an output per cylinder of 146bhp compared with 125bhp in the Class 40 engine. This enabled the company to offer a 1,750hp locomotive with a 12-cylinder engine and the Co-Co wheel arrangement within the weight range of 100-105 tons. This more powerful Type 3 unit was later classified as Class 37.

With an overall width of only 8ft 11.6in and an axle load of 17.5ton, the Class 37 locomotives can run over nearly all BR routes. Steam-heating boilers were fitted at first but many have been removed. The generator group was specifically designed to allow later conversion to electric heating by installing a heating generator between the main and auxiliary machines. In the swing bolster bogies, stirrups for the underslung equalising beams are incorporated in the roller bearing axleboxes. The locomotives are a characteristic Vulcan Foundry product, similar in appearance to Class 40 apart from the six-wheel bogies. The power equipment differed from previous designs from the English Electric Group in having an oil servo-operated load regulator instead of a pilot motor drive. When allocated to the Western Region, the writing was on the wall for the diesel-hydraulics. Pairs of '37s' geared for high speed were used during investigations for an accelerated Paddington-West of England timetable in 1965, and in 1976 the locomotives were used in threes on 1,000ton iron ore trains for Llanwern steelworks – a working described as 'BR's heaviest freight train'. Their use on BR is widespread on passenger and freight work and they have been particularly identified with main line services from Liverpool Street. The life of Class 37 has been extended by an estimated 20 years by rebuilding 31 locomotives with main and auxiliary alternators in place of the present dc equipment. Deliveries of the rebuilds commenced during 1985. These locomotives are also fitted for electric train-heating and designated Class 37/4.

Above:
The earlier Type 3 English Electric locomotives of Class 37 were built with end gangway doors and split headcode boxes on either side. D6778 retains green livery together with full yellow ends in this view, passing through York station with the 12.50 Tees Yard-New England freight on 29 August 1970. *D. Wharton*

Right:
One of the later Class 37s built without gangway doors, enabling a tidier headcode panel to be fitted, No 6856 passes Polmadie depot Glasgow with a block oil train on 7 September 1971 in clean BR blue livery. *N. E. Preedy*

Class 40

Number series: D200-D399†
Engine: English Electric 16SVT MkII
Cylinders: Sixteen, 10in × 12in
Rating: 2,000hp at 850rpm
Transmission: Six EE nose-suspended traction motors
Maximum speed: 90mph

Wheel arrangement: 1Co-Co1
Driving wheel dia: 3ft 9in
Continuous TE: 30,900lb at 18mph
Maximum TE: 52,000lb
Weight: 133ton
First loco built: March 1958

† Later renumbered 40.001-40.199

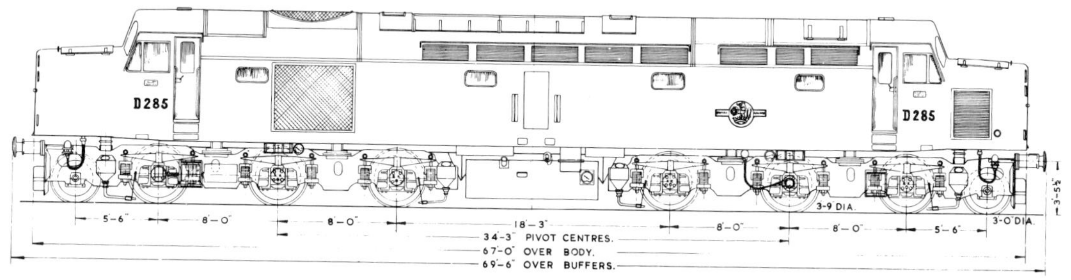

Top:
General arrangement of 2,000hp Class 40 diesel-electric 1Co-Co1. *R. S. Carter*

Above:
English Electric Type 4, later Class 40, No D210 *Empress of Britain* stands at Euston station on the occasion of its naming ceremony on 12 May 1960. The locomotive is in original all over green livery and has folding indicator discs. The large eight wheel bogies, with leading non-powered carrying axle will be noted. *BR (LM)*

The first diesel-electric locomotives for main line passenger work to go into service under the modernisation plan were the 2,000hp Class 40s. They were powered by the Mk II version of the English Electric 16SVT engine as already installed in the third of the Southern Region's diesel-electrics, No 10203. Another feature inherited from the Southern design were the eight-wheel bogies with three powered axles and a weight-carrying pony truck within the bogie frame, giving the locomotives the 1Co-Co1 wheel arrangement. The absence of secondary suspension, the body being carried directly on the bogies by segmental bearings, added to traction motor problems by hard riding, and the primary springs

Left:
The final Class 40s to be constructed, like the later Class 37s, were fitted with integral headcode panels, central gangway doors being dispensed with. No D385 heads the down 'Royal Scot' between Tebay and Scout Green on 12 April 1963.
J. S. Whiteley

Below:
In later years the Class 40s were relegated more to freight duties rather than express passenger. No 40.133 in final blue livery with yellow ends has charge of an eastbound oil train at Manchester Victoria on 1 May 1981. The locomotive features the intermediate design with split headcode boxes, by now no longer used for their original purpose.
J. C. Hillmer

were later modified. The difficulty had been a tendency to flashovers when working at high speed in weak field, caused partly by vibration and partly by the conditions in which the motors were operating, due to a gear ratio chosen both for high tractive effort and 90mph maximum speed. Four-pole motors were later substituted for the original six-pole version. Motor grouping was three parallel circuits of two machines in series.

Styling was an improvement on the Southern diesel-electrics, the nose ends, containing auxiliary equipment, emphasising an impressive overall length of 69ft 6in, to which the centipede effect of eight axles added interest although betraying a poor ratio of power to weight. The laminated springs of the axlebox suspension had the familiar look of steam locomotive tender springing, and were reassuring in a period when there was still something extra-terrestrial about a diesel locomotive. All locomotives were equipped for working in multiple and doors were provided in the nose ends so that the crew could pass from one locomotive to the next if necessary. Four-digit train description indicators had to be split into two, with two digits on each side of the doors, but in practice the doors were little used and were omitted in later builds, those which remained being welded up. Single-unit indicators showing all four digits could then be fitted but were eventually phased out and marker lights were carried. Originally the locomotives were fitted with discs for showing the earlier form of headcodes, which indicated the class of a train but not its identity.

Apart from one short-lived trial installation, the class was not converted for electric train heating. All locomotives were built with train heating boilers but many of them were removed as the class was superseded on regular passenger duties by later designs of higher power. On long passenger runs the heating water supply could be replenished from track water troughs, a scoop being fitted to the tank on the underframe.

By late 1984 only a few members of Class 40 were left in service, and all were withdrawn by February 1985 except 40.122 (originally D200), retained for use on railtours.

Classes 44, 45 and 46

Number series: D1-D10†
Engine: Sulzer 12LDA28-A
Cylinders: Twelve, 11.02in × 14.2in
Rating: 2,300hp at 750rpm
Transmission: Six Crompton Parkinson axle-hung, nose-suspended traction motors
Maximum speed: 90mph

Wheel arrangement: 1Co-Co1
Driving wheel dia: 3ft 9in
Continuous TE: 41,000lb at 16.5mph
Maximum TE: 70,000lb
Weight: 133ton
First loco built: September 1959
Last loco withdrawn: November 1980

Below:
General arrangement of 2,300hp Class 44 diesel-electric 1Co-Co1.

† Later renumbered 44.001-44.010

Number series: D11-D137†
Engine: Sulzer 12LDA28-B
Cylinders: Twelve, 11.02in × 14.2in
Rating: 2,500hp at 750rpm
Transmission: Six Crompton Parkinson axle-hung, nose-suspended traction motors
Maximum speed: 90mph

Wheel arrangement: 1Co-Co1
Driving wheel dia: 3ft 9in
Continuous TE: 41,000lb at 16.15mph
Maximum TE: 70,000lb
Weight: 136ton
First loco built: October 1960

† Later renumbered 45.001-45.077, 45.101-45.150

Below:
General arrangement of 2,500hp Class 45 diesel-electric 1Co-Co1.

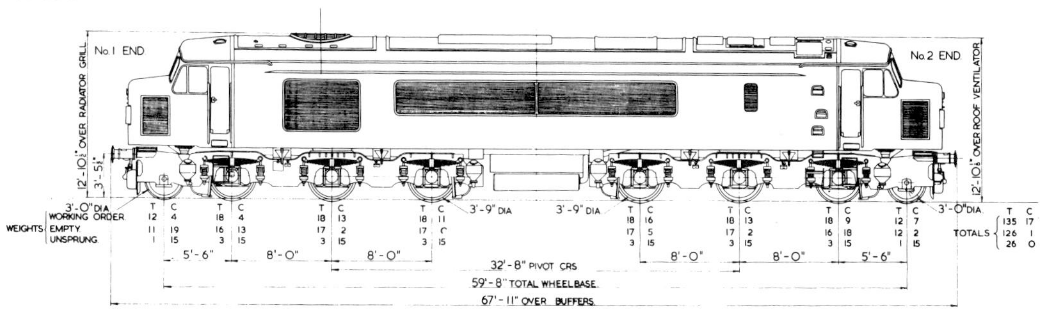

Number series: D138-D193†
Engine: Sulzer 12LDA28-B
Cylinders: Twelve
Rating: 2,500hp
Transmission: Six Brush axle-hung, nose-suspended traction motors
Maximum speed: 90mph

Wheel arrangement: 1Co-Co1
Driving wheel dia: 3ft 9in
Continuous TE: 41,000lb at 16.5mph
Maximum TE: 70,000lb
Weight: 138ton
First loco built: November 1961
Last loco withdrawn:

† Later renumbered 46.001-46.056

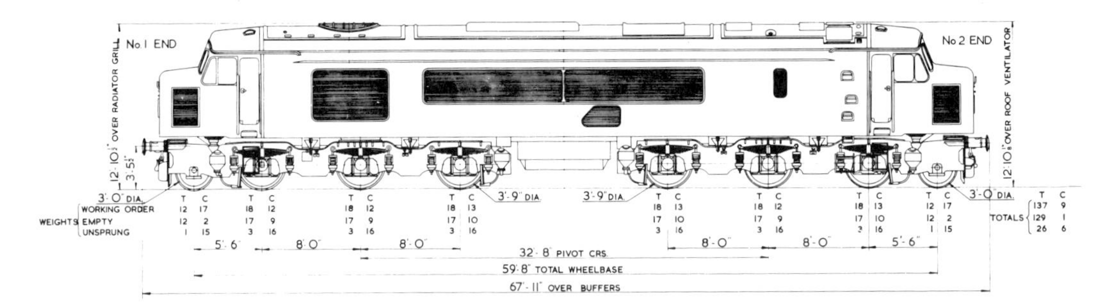

These closely allied locomotive classes are often referred to collectively as 'Peaks' although the true 'Peaks' were the 10 locomotives of Class 44 which were named after mountains in the British Isles. Appearance of the class was awaited with interest, for this was British Rail's own venture into design for higher powers. When all was revealed, there were mixed feelings. The Derby-built locomotive had the traditional but somewhat stunted nose ends and a multiplicity of wheels. It was, indeed, endowed with the Bulleid type of bogie with three motored axles and a pony truck, as first seen in the three Southern main line diesel-electrics and carried on in Class 40. For a weight of 138 tons it produced 2,300hp from its Sulzer engine, and a contemporary technical publication hailed it unenthusiastically as a 'Heavy general-purpose design with one engine'. The engine was the 12-cylinder Sulzer 12LDA28 with two banks of six cylinders and two crankshafts driving the generator group through gearing. At the rated engine speed of 750rpm the generator speed was 1,080rpm.

The pony truck in each bogie rotated about a virtual pivot under the guidance of two pairs of links with spherical bearings anchored to the buffer beam. It was loaded by spherical-seated bearers and controlled by side springs. Traction motors were axle-hung, and the centre motored axle was allowed side play, the motor moving with it, a degree of 'float' being allowed by the sandwich type rubbers of the nose suspension. Motors on the outer axles had chevron type rubber nose suspension which limited sideways movement. The motors were connected in parallel and had five steps of field weakening. Electrical equipment was supplied by Crompton Parkinson Ltd who used their characteristic form of generator construction with the auxiliary generator recessed into the armature of

Above:
General arrangement of 2,500hp Class 46 diesel-electric 1Co-Co1.

Below:
First of the 'Peaks', No D1 *Scafell Pike* poses for a publicity photograph when new in 1959. The 10 members of Class 44 were built with folding headcode discs instead of the later headcode panels. *BR (LM)*

Top right:
Class 45 No D84 *Royal Corps of Transport* fitted with the twin box heacode panels hauls a Derby-Manchester express 'wrong line' due to bridge maintenance at Grindleford on 11 February 1972. *L. A. Nixon*

Above right:
Many of the later 'Peak' type locomotives were fitted with central headcode panels as in this view of Class 46 No 46.024 on an empty stone working on 7 March 1974 leaving Salisbury. The members of Class 46 had Brush electrical equipment. *G. F. Gillham*

the main machine, which had its commutator at the driving end. The auxiliary generator field magnets were attached to the end shield of the combined machine.

The weight of the Class 44 locomotive in relation to its horsepower was a talking point for advocates of diesel-hydraulic traction, who were vocal at that time. An improvement was on the way, however, for an intercooled version of the Sulzer 12LDA28 engine had been developed which increased the output to 2,500hp. A further series of locomotives to the same general design as Class 44 was ordered, but powered by the 12LDA28-B intercooled engine. Construction was shared by Crewe and Derby and the locomotives were designated Class 45, the first going into service in 1960. Crompton Parkinson again supplied the electrical equipment. A change was made in the auxiliary system, the auxiliary generator being a 220V machine. The normal 110V control supply was provided by a 220/110V rotary converter. Traction motors were smaller than in Class 44, lowering the starting tractive effort from 70,000lb to 55,000lb, but a Class 45 locomotive was still able to start a train of 1,000 tons on a 1 in 100 gradient.

Class 46 followed in 1961, again to the same mechanical design but now with Brush electrical equipment and a change in the motor grouping from six machines in parallel to three parallel pairs of two in series.

Locomotives of all three classes were built with heating boilers. The 44s lost theirs in 1962 and were

Above:
The appearance of many Class 45 and 46 locomotives was significantly altered from the late 1970s by removal of the redundant headcode panels which were replaced by two marker lights. No 45.104 *The Lancashire Fusilier*, seen ascending the Lickey incline with the 07.30 Swansea-Leeds on 13 November 1980 is a member of Class 45/1 which are fitted with electric train heating equipment. *A. O. Wynn*

put on to freight duties. In 1974 the boilers were removed from 50 Class 45s and alternators replaced the auxiliary generators, providing both control and train heating supplies through rectifiers. The ETH locomotives became Class 45/1 and the others 45/0. Class 46 kept their boilers but the decline of steam-heating made them early targets for storage and withdrawal. The 'Peaks' replaced steam on the St Pancras main line, giving a shot in the arm to its services and becoming as typical of that terminus as the Midland Compounds had been in their day. They were also prominent on major cross-country routes and held in high esteem in spite of their rather ponderous image (or perhaps because of it?).

Being less successful than Classes 45 and 46. and also being a non-standard class of only ten members, the 44s were obvious candidates for withdrawal and by the end of 1980 the class was extinct. Class 46 followed with the last example being withdrawn in late 1984.

Class 47

Number series: D1100-D1111, D1500-D1999†
Engine: Sulzer 12LDA28-C
Cylinders: Twelve
Rating: 2,580hp at 750rpm*
Transmission: Six Brush axle-hung, nose-suspended traction motors
Maximum speed: 95mph, 47/7: 100mph

Wheel arrangement: Co-Co
Wheel dia: 3ft 9in
Continuous TE: 30,000lb at 27mph
Maximum TE: 55,000lb
Weight: 111ton-125ton
First loco built: September 1962

* Originally 2,750hp at 800rpm
† Later renumbered as 47.001-47.901
Note: D1702-D1706 originally built as Class 48 with Sulzer 12LVA24 engines rated 2,650hp at 1,050rpm

---

Class 47/9
Engine: Ruston 12RK3ACT
Cylinders: Twelve
Rating: 3,300hp at 1,000rpm

Maximum TE: 58,000lb
Weight: 116ton

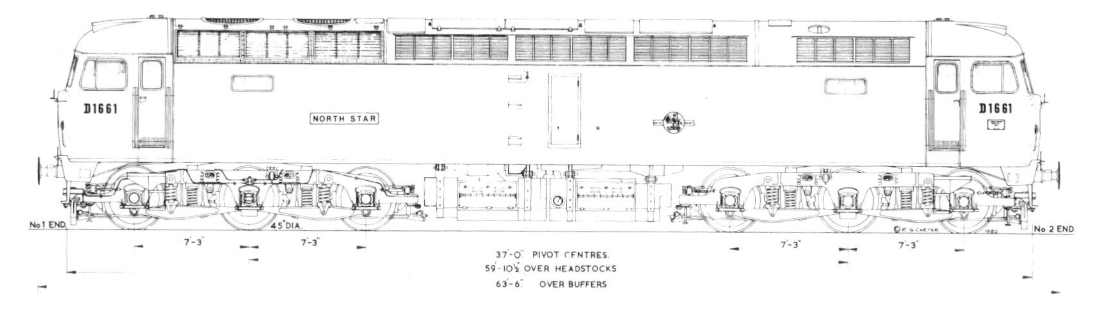

Above:
General arrangement of 2,580hp Class 47 diesel-electric Co-Co. *R. S. Carter*

Below:
The most numerous main line locomotive on BR is the Class 47, of which 512 examples were built. Seen here is the attractive original two-tone green livery. No D1714 stands at the buffers at Paddington with the 14.35 from Birkenhead on 7 April 1964. *B. Stephenson*

At the beginning of the 1960s British Railways were looking for a more powerful general-purpose main line diesel with a shorter bogie wheelbase than current designs in that category. Three prototypes were on trial, one of them with a 2,750hp version of the 2,500hp Sulzer engine in Classes 45 and 46. The Brush Electrical Engineering Company of Loughborough had submitted a 2,800hp locomotive with two high-speed engines, but BR's preference was for a medium-speed diesel. But the Brush company offered good prospects of continuity of production and had developed a lightweight method of body construction. Although its high-speed engine proposal was turned down, the company was awarded a contract for building a new design of locomotive powered by the Sulzer 2,750hp engine. This was the beginning of the most numerous class of large diesel locomotives on British Railways, known at first as the Brush Type 4 and later as Class 47.

In Classes 44 to 46 the bogies had three motored axles and a separate carrying axle in a pony truck within the bogie frames. Class 47 had two three-axle bogies with all axles motored. The integral construction of body and underframe as a single unit kept the axle-load within the limits laid down. In the Sulzer 12LDA28-C engine two banks of six vertical cylinders each drove a separate crankshaft and the crankshafts were geared to a single output shaft. At the rated engine speed of 800rpm the output shaft speed was 1,152rpm. The generator group was coupled to the output shaft.

In the first 20 locomotives the traction and train-heating armatures were within the main generator frame, and the auxiliary generator frame was bolted to the end plate. A train-heating boiler was carried for steam-heated rolling stock. At first the requirement for electric train-heating was limited and further locomotives were built with main and auxiliary generators only. With the introduction of electrically-heated and air-conditioned rolling stock, however, more locomotives with a train-heating output were required. It was provided by replacing the auxiliary

generator with an alternator and taking two ac outputs from its stator, one for auxiliaries in the locomotive and the other for train heating. Both outputs were rectified.

The locomotives were carried on cast steel bogies with swing bolsters and axlebox guides. Underslung equalising beams linked the axleboxes and carried the coil springs of the primary suspension. Secondary suspension between spring planks and bolster was also by coil springs. Roller suspension bearings carried the traction motors on

Above:
The general purpose use of most modern diesels which particularly characterises the Class 47s is shown in this view of No 47.157 on a train of empty stone hoppers about to enter the down loop at Hungerford on 19 May 1977. *G. F. Gillham*

Below:
A Glasgow-Edinburgh push-pull train approaches Edinburgh Waverley on 19 June 1981 with No 47.711 *Greyfriars Bobby*, equipped for remote control from a driving trailer when pushing. *C. J. Tuffs*

the axles, and the motor nose suspension was by short links with rubber-bushed attachments to the motor 'nose' and bogie transoms. In the earlier locomotives the motors were connected in three parallel pairs of two in series but later builds changed to six motors in parallel, with a lower-voltage main generator.

As a result of problems with the diesel engines in the mid-1960s, traced in part to high stresses on certain components, various modifications were made and the engine speed was reduced to 750rpm, with a rating of 2,580hp. Control gear has been modified in various respects in step with developments in technology and the locomotives have been equipped with low-speed control for use in working merry-go-round (MGR) trains through automatic unloading plant at collieries. The whole class was scheduled in 1976 to undergo a Heavy General Repair programme to extend their working life, now expected to go into the 1990s.

Twelve locomotives were adapted for remote control from a driving trailer and in 1980 took over from Class 27s on Glasgow-Edinburgh push-pull services. The control system uses the two train lighting wires for transmission of coded high-speed pulse signals to the locomotive. These signals select four levels of air pressure for setting the governor, providing four engine speeds. These 12 locomotives form Class 47/7. A further four Class 47/7 locomotives were converted from 47/4 in 1984/5.

In 1974 No 47.046 was converted as a mobile test bed for the diesel engine and alternator transmission system to be used in the Class 56 freight locomotives. It was renumbered 47.601 and classified 47/6. When a 12-cylinder version of the Class 56 engine was produced, No 47.601 was again used as a mobile test bed, and on emerging from works with the new engine was renumbered 47.901. The 12-cylinder engine became the power unit of the Class 58 freight locomotives.

Five Class 47s were selected for testing a vee version of the Sulzer LDA engine. They formed Class 48 but after the necessary service experience had been gained they were re-engined with the LDA diesel and reverted to Class 47.

Class 50

Number series: D400-D449†
Engine: English Electric 16CSVT
Cylinders: Sixteen
Rating:2,700hp at 850rpm
Transmission: Six E.E. axle-hung, nose-suspended traction motors
Maximum speed: 100mph

Wheel arrangement: Co-Co
Wheel dia: 3ft 7in
Continuous TE: 33,000lb at 23.5mph
Maximum TE: 48,500lb
Weight: 115ton
First loco built: September 1967

† Later renumbered 50.001-50.050

Below:
General arrangement of 2,700hp Class 50 diesel-electric Co-Co.

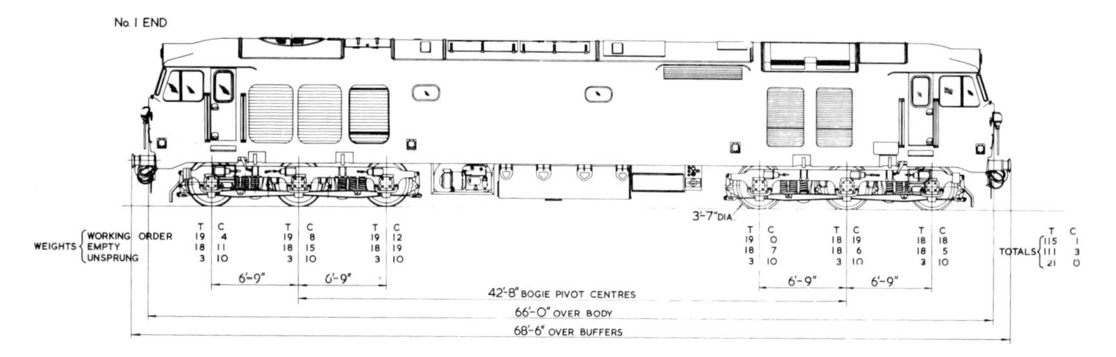

When BR was looking for a main line diesel-electric of more than 2,000hp, the English Electric Company put forward a Co-Co with a 2,700hp rating. This locomotive, DP2, was handed over to BR for trial running in April 1962. It operated in the London Midland and Eastern Regions until its career was cut short by a collision in 1967, and it was broken up in the following year. DP2 was an advanced design in many respects and formed the basis of the later BR Class 50 locomotives which were powered by the same engine and main generator as the prototype.

The diesel engine in DP2 and Class 50 was the English Electric 16SVT giving 2,700hp at 850rpm. It was direct-coupled to the main generator, but the auxiliary generator was overhung from a train-heating generator, these two machines forming a separate group coupled to the main generator by a short cardan shaft. Mechanical design followed BR specifications, so that the characteristic English Electric nose end, prominent in DP2, gave place to a flat-ended superstructure. The swing bolster bogies were similar to those in Classes 37 and 55, with underslung equalising beams carrying the axleboxes. Traction motors were also similar to the Classes 37 and 55 machines. For the first time in BR diesel practice the locomotives were equipped for dynamic (rheostatic) braking.

Main generator excitation was controlled electronically by a closed loop system that adjusted speed and tractive effort according to the driver's manipulation of the power handle. If he called for a higher effort than admissible in the adhesion conditions a lower value was imposed, and if wheelspin had begun it was quickly corrected. The driver could also preset a particular tractive effort which would be held constant during acceleration. An automatic low-speed control for use of merry-go-round workings was included in the system.

Class 50s were soon put on to double-heading LMR Anglo-Scottish expresses north of Crewe or Preston while electrification was being extended northwards from Weaver Junction. When this work was completed, they were transferred to the Western Region, where availability suffered from various generator and traction motor faults. In 1979 a programme of refurbishing and modifying the whole class was undertaken. Some equipment which had proved unnecessary had already been disconnected and was now removed, including the rheostatic brake unit. The space made available enabled the inertial air filtration to be replaced by more efficient oil-damped filters, reducing contamination inside the locomotive which had been a source of electrical troubles. The pre-set tractive effort and low-speed controls were also removed, and the control electronics were updated with new circuit boards and components. A headlamp was fitted in the centre of the panel below the cab windows. From the seventh refurbished locomotive onwards they were turned out from the works in the new-style BR livery with all-yellow cab and enlarged BR logo and numerals, the logo occupying the full depth of the bodysides.

Originally the Class 50s were not purchased by BR but operated under a leasing agreement. This arrangement was terminated and the whole class bought by BR in the mid-1970s.

Above:
When first built the Class 50s were intended primarily for West Coast main line passenger duties as in this view of No 434 at Greenholme with a down Motorail service on 17 July 1971. The locomotive is in the early standard BR blue livery. *G. T. Heavyside*

Above right:
After the electrification of the WCML, the Class 50 fleet was transferred to the Western Region in place of the Class 52 diesel-hydraulics. No 50.020, named *Revenge* since its arrival on the WR departs from Woking on 15 May 1981 with the 11.10 Waterloo-Exeter, now refurbished and carrying the new livery with yellow cabs, and large numbers and double arrow. *C. J. Marsden*

Class 53 *Falcon*

Number series: 1200†
Engines: Two Maybach MD655
Cylinders: Twelve, 7.28in × 7.88in
Rating: 1,400hp at 1,500rpm
Transmission: Six Brush traction motors
Maximum speed: 100mph

Wheel arrangement: Co-Co
Wheel dia: 3ft 7in
Continuous TE: 28,500lb at 28.5mph
Maximum TE: 50,000lb
Weight: 115ton
Loco built: September 1961
Loco withdrawn: October 1975

† Originally D0280

Below:
General arrangement of 2,800hp Class 53 diesel-electric Co-Co No 1200 *Falcon*. *R. S. Carter*

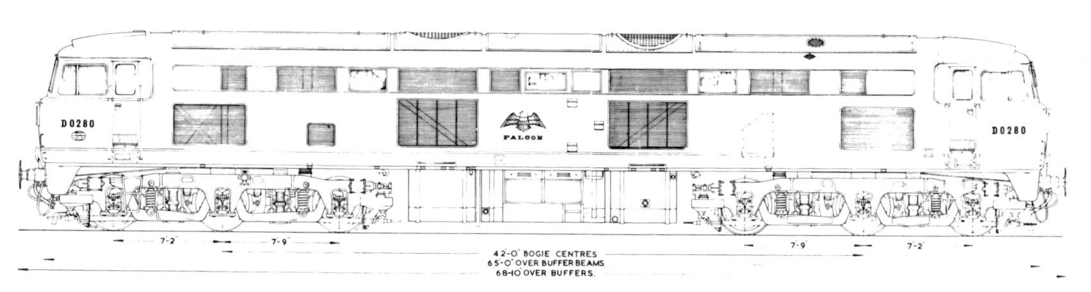

While other builders were looking to intercooled medium-speed diesel engines for outputs of 2,500hp and upwards, the Brush Electrical Engineering Co Ltd borrowed the diesel-hydraulic concept of two high-speed diesels but put them into a locomotive with electric transmission. The company's *Falcon* prototype was a Co-Co of 2,800hp weighing 115ton and with a power/weight ratio of 24hp/ton came close to the 25hp/ton of contemporary diesel-hydraulics on the Western Region.

The engines were the Bristol-Siddeley Maybach MD655 giving 1,400hp at 1,500rpm and the power equipment was planned as two separate units mounted on one frame so that in the event of one set of equipment failing, 1,400hp would still be available. Each engine was direct-coupled to a main generator supplying power independently to three traction motors. Auxiliary generators were mounted on top of the main machines and belt-driven and each was coupled to a traction motor blower. Normally the auxiliary machines worked in parallel

Above:
With BR numbering and standard blue livery, No 1200 *Falcon* is about to leave Paddington with the 10.45 to Weston-super-Mare on 16 June 1972. *G. F. Gillham*

to supply the total load, but if one power unit failed, all auxiliaries could be operated at half power from the other. Three stages of traction motor field-weakening enabled the full engine power to be utilised up to 100mph.

The locomotive undertook trial running on BR with the running number D0280. In tests on the Western Region it started smoothly with 568ton on the 1 in 36 to 1 in 45 gradients west of Newton Abbot. Speeds attained on the level were 100mph with 273ton and 75mph with an 18-coach train weighing 600ton. In a further test on the Lickey Incline the locomotive made a smooth start from standstill with a load of 628ton (20 vehicles).

In 1962 *Falcon* began a regular turn of duty in the Eastern Region on the 'Master Cutler' King's Cross-Sheffield Pullman express, normally making two round trips totalling 670 miles every 24 hours. Freight working followed with loads of 800 to 1,100ton between Whitemoor and Mansfield before the locomotive was returned to the Brush works in 1963. Two years later *Falcon* was back at work on the Western Region, where its MD655 engines were already familiar in the 'Western' class diesel-hydraulic. Here the locomotive operated both express passenger turns and general duties appropriate to its Class 4 rating. In 1970 *Falcon* was taken into BR stock with the number D1200 but was withdrawn in 1975 and scrapped in the following year.

Class 55 'Deltic'

Number series: D9000-D9021†
Engines: Two Napier 18-25 Deltic
Cylinders: Eighteen, 5.125in × 7.25in
Rating: 1,650hp at 1,500rpm
Transmission: Six EE axle-hung, nose-suspended traction motors
Maximum speed: 100mph
Wheel arrangement: Co-Co
Wheel dia: 3ft 7in
Continuous TE: 30,500lb at 32.5mph
Maximum TE: 50,000lb
Weight: 99ton
First loco built: March 1961
Last loco withdrawn: January 1982

† Later renumbered as 55.001-55.022

Below:
General arrangement of 3,300hp Class 55 diesel-electric Co-Co.

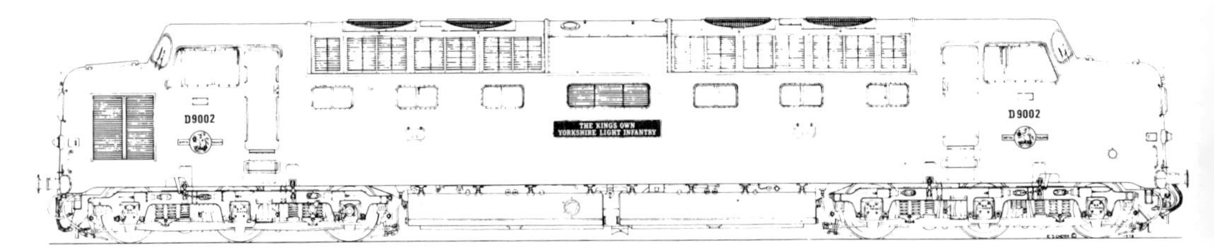

A 3,300hp diesel-electric locomotive weighing only 106ton was a phenomenon in the autumn of 1955. These were the vital statistics of the English Electric Company's prototype Co-Co *Deltic* which made its appearance in that year (see Chapter 8, Experimental Locomotives). In a period when the traditional traction diesel in Britain was a heavy machine giving its rated output at between 700 and 800rpm, *Deltic* was powered by two engines giving 1,650hp at 1,500rpm, built with many light alloy components. Light alloys and other methods of saving weight were employed in the construction of the locomotive.

Between 1955 and 1961 *Deltic* travelled more than 400,000 miles in the London Midland, Eastern and Scottish Regions, remaining the property of the English Electric Company throughout. British Rail policy at that time inclined towards single-engined locomotives with general-purpose characteristics, and *Deltic* was designed specifically as a high-speed passenger unit. This was exactly what the general manager of the Eastern Region was looking for to implement his plans for accelerated services on the East Coast main line and he was successful in obtaining sanction from the British Transport Commission for an order for 22 locomotives based on the prototype. All were built at English Electric's Vulcan Foundry plant. Delivered between April 1959 and March 1962, they formed the celebrated fleet known later as Class 55.

A distinctive feature of the prototype was the construction of the bolsters so that they formed ducts for distributing cooling air to the traction motors. Air from the blowers entered through the hollow pivots, which did not carry the body weight, this being borne by the side bearers. A similar system was used in the Class 37 bogies, and again in the bogies of the production 'Deltics', which were interchangeable with those of Class 37. The bogie wheelbase was 13ft 6in, compared with 14ft 4in of the prototype, giving wider route availability. In the secondary suspension, coil springs replaced transverse elliptical springs but the primary suspension was unchanged, the axleboxes being linked by underslung equalising beams which carried coil springs supporting the bogie frame. The production locomotives were 5ft 6in longer over buffers than the prototype but perhaps the most remarkable achievement of the revised design was the reduction in weight to only 99ton.

Changes in the electrical design included self-ventilated main generators, eliminating two motor-blowers, and step-down gears to the output shafts so that the generators ran at 1,125rpm with the engines on full power instead of at the engine speed of 1,500rpm. In contrast with most BR diesel-electric locomotives the auxiliary generators were gear-driven at 1.67 times engine speed instead of being overhung on the main generator shafts.

Below:
Class 55 'Deltic' No D9010 *The King's Own Scottish Borderer* stands in spotless blue livery after overhaul. For many years these were the most powerful diesel locomotives on BR and responsible for East Coast main line express services.

The locomotives were geared for a maximum speed of 105mph.

Today the 'Deltic roar' is remembered with affection. It was less appreciated by the engine crews who had to listen to it close behind their backs for hours on end, and considerable trouble and expense was involved in improving the sound-proofing of cabs. In later years the provision of power for electric train heating and air-conditioning was another problem. There was no room for auxiliary alternators in line with the main generators, and even if there had been, there was no provision for extending the main generator shafts to carry the additional rotors. The heating/air-conditioning supply had therefore to be taken from the main generators themselves, with the difficulty that voltage fell appreciably when the locomotive was running easily with the engines throttled back. In the system eventually adopted, both generators were able to supply the heating load but in normal running it was taken from one only. With the engines idling, however, both generators were fully excited and operated in series to provide 850V. This condition obtained in stations and when the locomotive was coasting for more than a few seconds.

On applying power, the train heating supply was switched off and not restored until at least 600V were being supplied for traction. From that stage onwards one generator supplied both ETH and traction power while the other supplied traction power only. The formations of 'Deltic'-hauled trains of air-conditioned stock did not vary greatly and these supply arrangements proved adequate.

In 1968 the Eastern Region introduced a number of fast business services formed of eight-coach trains hauled by Class 55 locomotives. The timetable columns showed them as 'High Speed' and with hindsight the words can be seen as foretelling the future. Later the trains were given 'Executive' titles, and from 1979 the Leeds, Bradford and Newcastle 'Executives' became 'High Speed Trains' in two senses, being worked by Class 254 HSTs. The 'Hull Executive' remained a Class 55 duty until 2 January 1981. When accelerated in 1979 this service became the fastest locomotive-hauled train on British Railways with an average speed of 91.32mph from King's Cross to Retford.

Class 56

Number series: 56.001-56.135
Engine: Ruston 16RK3CT
Cylinders: Sixteen
Rating:3,250hp at 900rpm
Transmission: Six Brush traction motors
Maximum speed: 80mph

Wheel arrangement: Co-Co
Wheel dia: 3ft 9in
Continuous TE: 54,000lb at 17mph
Maximum TE: 61,000lb
Weight: 126ton
First loco built: August 1976

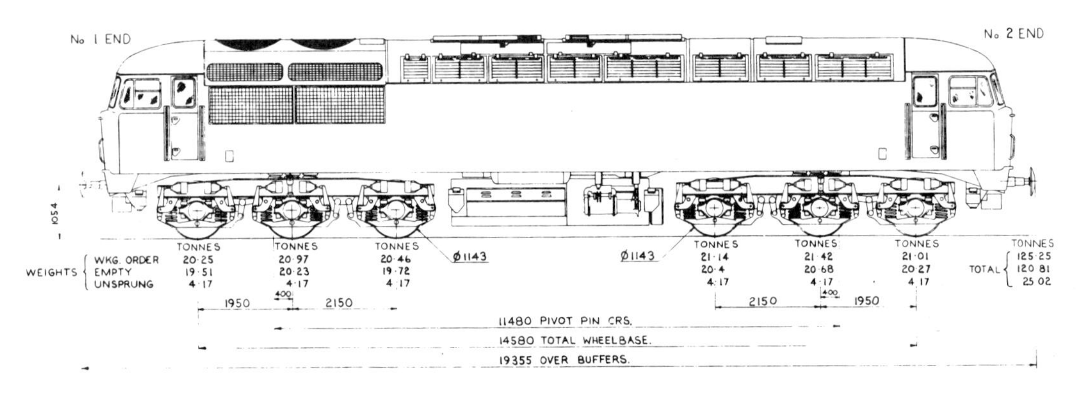

Above:
General arrangement of 3,250hp Class 56 diesel-electric Co-Co.

When outputs in the 3,000hp range are required from a diesel-electric locomotive a dc generator is reaching the limits of acceptable commutation. Current BR practice for all new diesel-electric motive power is for the diesel engine to drive the rotor of an alternator, the ac being collected through fixed contacts from the stator winding and rectified externally. The rotor is a revolving electromagnet and so has to be excited with dc. An exciter alternator is coupled to the rotor shaft and its output is converted to dc by diodes mounted on the shaft and revolving with it. There are no sliding contacts through brushgear and so the whole arrangement is called a 'brushless alternator'.

Above:
Romanian-built Class 56 No 56.017 thunders towards Shireoaks East Junction with an MGR train from Seymour Junction to Cottam power station on 30 May 1978.
B. J. Nicolle

Apart from the brushless alternator in the prototype 4,000hp locomotive *Kestrel*, this type of machine did not come into use on BR until the prototype HST of 1972. It was next adopted for the heavy freight locomotives of Class 56. Earlier main-line diesels had generally been designed with mixed traffic duties in view. Class 56 was specifically for heavy freight, particularly merry-go-round trains between collieries and power stations. The locomotive was powered by an English Electric 16RK3CT diesel engine in direct lineal descent from those in the pioneer main line diesels Nos 10000 and 10001, but now developing over twice the power for a lower weight in pounds per horsepower. In Class 56 the setting was 3,250hp at 900rpm.

The main contractor for these powerful Co-Co locomotives was Brush Electrical Machines Ltd but to meet BR delivery requirements arrangements were made for the first 30 to be assembled at the Craiova works of the Electroputere company in Romania. A further 30 followed from Doncaster. Deliveries of Romania-built locomotives began in 1976, and of those from Doncaster in 1977. In the British batch there were several changes in structural design to reduce the cost of construction. The cab structure was simplified, using heavier gauge steel instead of the original aluminium. Building of later batches, bringing the total in the class to 135, continued to be at Doncaster until the last 20, which were built at Crewe.

The bogies are a characteristic feature, each axlebox having its own short equalising beam which spreads the load between the two coil springs supported by it. It is less easy to see the additional equaliser system in the shape of a beam from the top of the inner spring at the bufferbeam end of the bogie and the adjacent spring of the central axle. These arrangements, together with unequal spacing of the bogie axles, are designed to minimise transfer of weight between axles, and consequent loss of adhesion, when the locomotive is starting a heavy train. Secondary suspension is by flexicoil springs recessed into 'pockets' in the underframe so that they are not immediately obvious like the springs of the Class 86 and 87 electric locomotives.

The final member of the class No 56.135 entered service in November 1984. From 1984 for new construction of freight locomotives Class 56 was superseded by Class 58.

Class 58

Number series: 58.001-58.050
Engine: Ruston 12RK3ACT
Cylinders: Twelve
Rating: 3,300hp at 1,000rpm
Transmission: Six Brush traction motors
Maximum speed: 80mph

Wheel arrangement: Co-Co
Wheel dia: 3ft 8in
Continuous TE: 56,000lb at 14mph
Maximum TE: 60,000lb
Weight: 128ton
First loco built: May 1983

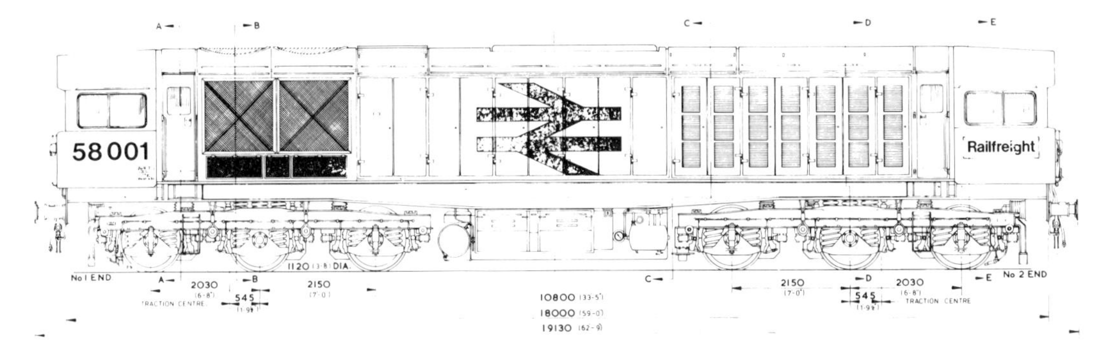

Class 56 followed the established body pattern of Class 47, but it was becoming increasingly expensive to build, while the power equipment occupied more space, with less room for access. It was therefore decided that a new and structurally simpler design would be necessary for further heavy freight power on BR. The answer was found by

Above:
General arrangement of 3,300hp Class 58 diesel-electric Co-Co. *R. S. Carter*

Below:
Class 58, Railfreight's 'workhorse'. No 58.002 takes the strain of its MGR load as it nears Drakelow power station on 11 November 1983. *A. O. Wynn*

putting the power equipment inside a 'bonnet' structure as had been done in Type 1 diesels at the beginning of the modernisation plan, but providing a cab at each end. This is the form of the Class 58 heavy freight locomotive, a Co-Co of 3,300hp. Power equipment is in four modular units between the cabs and accessible by removing the side and roof panels on the bonnet framework. The bogies, Type CP3, are a development of the CP2 bogies in Class 56, again with flexicoil suspension. Power comes from a Ruston-Paxman 12-cylinder engine with a rating in this application of 2,460kW (3,300hp) at 1,000rpm. Improvements in turbocharger performance and efficiency enable this engine to give a similar performance with fewer cylinders to that in Class 56, the output per cylinder being 291hp as compared with 218hp in Class 56.

The engine is coupled to an alternator and exciters, the electrical output for traction being rectified by 24 silicon diodes mounted on six heat sinks over which cooling air is drawn by a fan on the alternator shaft. The six traction motors are connected in three parallel pairs of two motors in series for normal running, but for low-speed operation under automatic control are connected all in series. Four slow-speed settings can be selected. The control system includes automatic correction of wheelslip. Class 58 locomotives can operate in multiple with each other but not with other classes.

The initial order for 35 locomotives was followed in 1984 by approval for a further 15 members of the class. Despite initial problems, particularly with poor performance of the wheelslip control, in late 1984 BR declared themselves satisfied with the Class 58s which were said to show a 15% saving on costs compared with Class 56.

Class 59

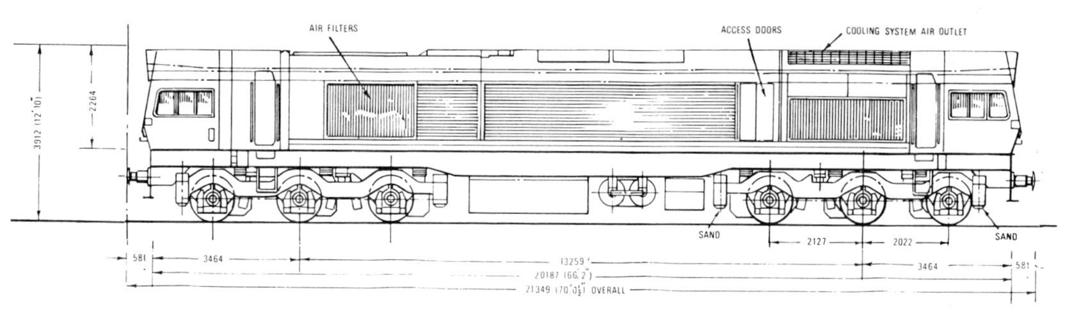

Above:
General arrangement of Foster Yeoman 3,300hp diesel-electric Co-Co.

In November 1984 the aggregate company Foster Yeoman Ltd announced that a £4 million order had been placed with General Motors of America to supply four diesel locomotives for the haulage of Foster Yeoman stone trains on British Rail. The locomotives would be 3,300hp Co-Co units of 121ton weight, delivery being due in December 1985. Each GM locomotive is expected to be able to do the work of two Class 56 or 58 locomotives, due to the American units' markedly higher adhesion factor, and expected availability.

These locomotives are the first privately owned locomotives to operate a regular service on the British Rail network; and in addition are the first American-built diesels to be used on the BR system. The units are intended specifically for use on Foster Yeoman traffic and are not part of the main BR fleet.

5 The Diesel Hydraulic Classes

Class 41 'Warship'

Number series: D600-D604
Engines: Two MAN L12V18/21A
Cylinders: Twelve, 7.1in × 8.3in
Rating: 1,000hp at 1,445rpm
Transmission: Two Voith-NBL L306r hydraulic transmissions
Maximum speed: 90mph
Wheel arrangement: A1A-A1A
Driving wheel dia: 3ft 7in
Continuous TE: 39,600lb at 12.6mph
Maximum TE: 49,460lb
Weight: 117ton 8cwt
First loco built: January 1958
Last loco withdrawn: December 1967

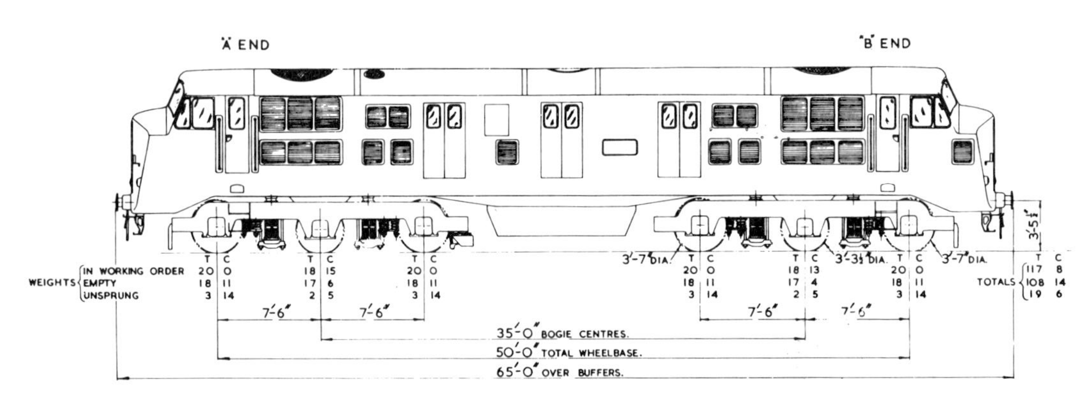

Above:
General arrangement of 2,000hp Class 41 diesel-hydraulic A1A-A1A.

In the early years of the BR modernisation plan, diesel locomotives with hydraulic transmission could show appreciably better ratios of power to weight than the average diesel-electric of the period. The V200 class B-B locomotive of the German Federal Railway, in service since 1953, weighed only 80 tons for 2,200hp while proposals for BR main line diesel-electrics suggested weights of over 100 tons in locomotives developing a modest 2,000hp. Certain characteristics of hydraulic transmission were particularly appropriate to traction requirements on the Western Region of British Railways. The Western Region Management successfully put a case to the British Transport Commission for the WR to become a testing ground for the diesel-hydraulic system when new locomotives were ordered.

The first WR diesel-hydraulics to go into service were five with the A1A-A1A wheel arrangement built by the North British Locomotive Co Ltd, and equipped with MAN engines and Voith transmissions. In three of the class both items were built by NBL under licence. The two diesel engines were set to give 1,000hp at 1,445rpm and each drove the two powered axles in one bogie through a Voith L306r transmission with three torque converters. A torque converter converts the power output of the diesel engine running at a constant speed so that the locomotive speed varies according to the changing load imposed by gradients and other factors. A single converter cannot be effective over the whole speed range of which a locomotive is capable, and so in the Voith system three converters with different characteristics took over from each other automatically at different track speeds. Cardan shaft drives coupled the engines to the transmission units, and the transmissions to the powered axles.

Above:
One of the five A1A-A1A 'Warships', No D601 *Ark Royal* heads the 'Royal Duchy' Paddington-Penzance express on 17 February 1958, the beat of its engine echoing from the banks of Sonning cutting.

Mechanical construction of the locomotives was in the substantial style favoured by the BTC engineers of the period and also in the tradition of a firm with a long and famous history of building steam locomotives. It did not provide a good example of diesel-hydraulic potential in the matter of power/weight ratio, the weight in working order amounting to a little over 117 tons.

The five locomotives were given the names of famous warships. The same theme was followed in the D800 series of B-B diesel-hydraulics which followed and it is to these that the name 'Warship' class is generally applied, their five predecessors forming the D600 class.

Class 22

Number series: D6300-D6357
Engine: MAN L12V18/21B
Cylinders: Twelve, 7.1in × 8.3in
Rating: 1,100hp at 1,530rpm*
Transmission: Voith-NBL L306r hydraulic transmission
Maximum speed: 75mph
Wheel arrangement: B-B
Wheel dia: 3ft 7in
Continuous TE: 30,000lb at 8mph
Maximum TE: 43,500lb*
Weight: 68ton
First loco built: January 1959
Last loco withdrawn: January 1972

* D6300-D6305 MAN L12V18/21A rated at 1,000hp at 1,445rpm. Maximum TE 45,000lb.

Below:
General arrangement of 1,100hp Class 22 diesel-hydraulic B-B.

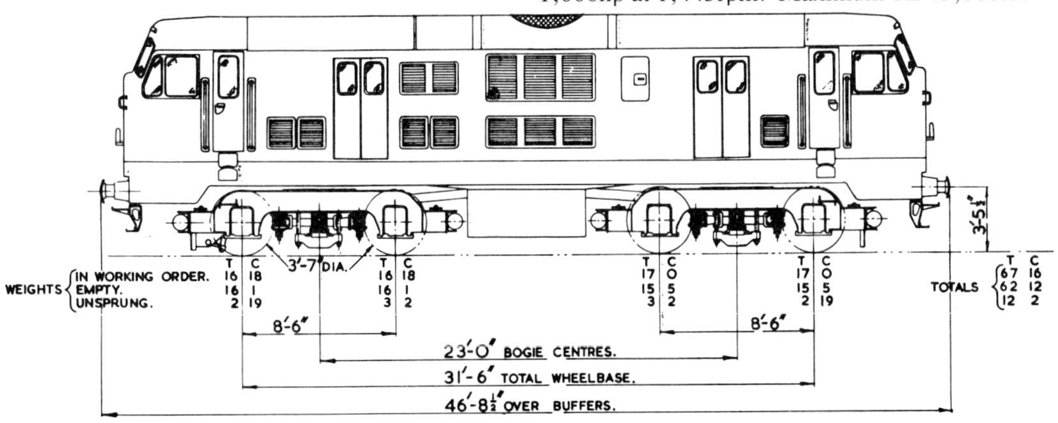

Above:
The NBL Type 2 diesel-hydraulics, later Class 22, were a single engine smaller version of the first 'Warships'. In its final condition in blue livery with yellow ends and fitted with twin headcode boxes, D6334 has charge of a china clay train at Petrockstow on 14 October 1969.

Six B-B diesel-hydraulic locomotives of 1,000hp were ordered for secondary duties on the Western Region at the same time as Class D600. They were again built by North British and had the NBL/MAN L12V18/21A engine and Voith L306r transmission, but with only one engine and transmission per locomotive. The transmission had an output coupling at each end with cardan shaft drives to the two axles of each bogie. Mechanical construction was on similar lines to the D600 class, the bogies being a two-axle version of the Class D600 three-axle bogie. Wheel diameter in both classes was 43in, there being no difference in diameter between the driving and carrying wheels in Class D600. After various modifications during construction the weight of the locomotives in working order was brought down to 68 tons.

Before any of the first six locomotives were delivered, an order was placed for 52 more similar locomotives, making this the largest diesel class ordered by BR up to that time. Although the locomotives were numbered consecutively and regarded as one class there were various differences between the first and second batches. While the first six had an electro-pneumatic control system and could work in multiple with the D600 class, the later ones had an all-electric system for compatability with the D800 class then under construction. For a similar reason the engine was the B version of the one in Nos D6300-5 and was set to 1,100hp at 1,530rpm. The transmission was the LT306r, which was more compact and lighter, and could handle a higher input power. Hydrostatic drive for the radiator fan replaced the electric drive which had been adopted in Class D600 and retained for the first six locomotives of Class D6300. Weight of this second batch of locomotives was 65 tons in working order.

Because of their restricted capability for multiple-unit control, the first six locomotives worked mainly in South Devon and Cornwall on light passenger and freight trains but were sometimes seen double-heading WR named expresses west of Plymouth. The later batch of 52 were widely dispersed over the WR system south of Birmingham.

Classes 42 and 43 'Warship'

Number series: D800-D832, D866-D870
Engines: Two Maybach MD650
Cylinders: Twelve, 7.3in × 7.8in
Rating: 1,135hp* at 1,530rpm
Transmission: Two Mekydro K104 hydraulic transmissions
Maximum speed: 90mph
Wheel arrangement: B-B
Wheel dia: 3ft 3.5in
Continuous TE: 45,000lb at 11.5mph
Maximum TE: 48,600lb
Weight: 78ton
First loco built: August 1958
Last loco withdrawn: December 1972

* D800-D802 engines rated at 1,056hp at 1,400rpm.

Note: D830
Engines: Two Paxman 12YJX
Cylinders: 7.75in × 8.5in
Rating: 1,200hp at 1,500rpm
Maximum TE: 47,780lb
Weight: 77ton 16cwt
Loco withdrawn: March 1969

Below:
General arrangement of 2,200hp Class 42 and 43 diesel-hydraulic 'Warship' B-B. *R. S. Carter*

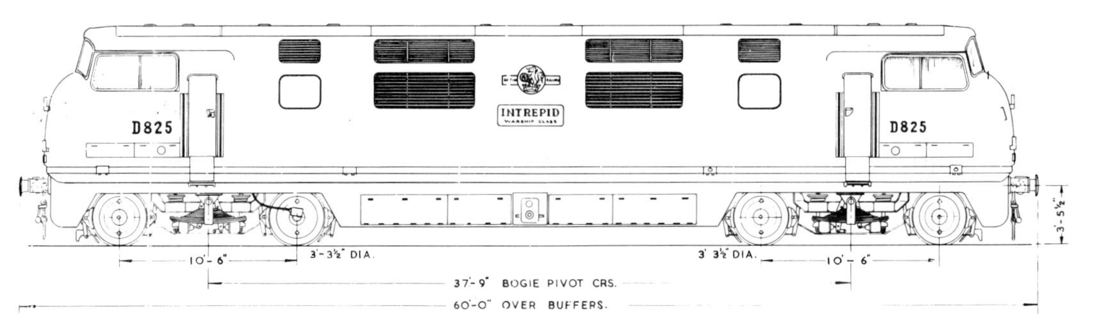

Number series: D833-D865
Engines: Two MAN L12V18/21B
Cylinders: Twelve, 7.1in × 8.3in
Rating: 1,100hp at 1,530rpm
Transmission: Two Voith-NBL LT306r hydraulic transmissions
Maximum speed: 90mph
Wheel arrangement: B-B
Wheel dia: 3ft 3.5in
Continuous TE: 37,000lb at 14mph
Maximum TE: 49,030lb
Weight: 79ton
First loco built: July 1960
Last loco withdrawn: October 1971

It was recognised that the mechanical construction of the Class D600 locomotives did not allow full advantage to be taken of the potential of diesel-hydraulic traction. The Western Region, therefore, investigated diesel-hydraulic practice in West Germany where the V200 B-B locomotive was earning a high reputation. It was decided that the future lay with a version of the V200 adapted to Western Region conditions, and agreements were concluded with West German manufacturers for diesel engines, transmissions and mechanical parts to be built under licence in Britain. The V200 was designed to take any of three makes of diesel engine and two types of transmission. Similar adaptability was postulated for the British version. The 'Warship' class locomotives beginning with D800 were therefore of two basic varieties, later classified by BR as Class 42 (Maybach engines and Mekydro transmissions) and Class 43 (MAN engines with Voith transmissions).

The Mekydro transmission had a single torque converter working in conjunction with a four-speed gearbox in which the ratios changed automatically in accordance with track speed. This was an alternative to the Voith three-converter system of providing the required characteristics over a wide locomotive speed range. At the moment of gear-change, the turbine wheel of the converter was shifted out of the main hydraulic circuit and slowed by the action of a secondary ring of fixed blades while dog clutches engaged the new ratio. Within a fraction of a second the change had been made and the turbine wheel moved back into position to resume the drive.

In the Maybach engines, the main crankshaft bearings were formed by the circular crank webs and corresponding circular apertures in the transverse crankcase stiffeners. The webs and the stiffener apertures were grooved to form races for the rollers. This construction was called a 'tunnel crankcase' because with the crankshaft removed the sequence of circular apertures inside the crankcase had the appearance of a tunnel.

Bogie design of the whole D800 series was distinctive. There was no bolster or pivot. The body was supported directly by inverted laminated springs, and its weight transferred to the bogie frame through coil springs and suspension links. The connection between body and bogie was by means of a system of rods and bell-cranks which

allowed rotation about a 'virtual' centre. In practice this arrangement gave insufficient freedom of lateral movement above 80mph and was later modified. The characteristic primary suspension remained unchanged, however, the roller bearing axleboxes being carried in arms pivoted from the centre transom, with plate springs between the outer (axlebox) ends of the arms and the bogie frame.

All locomotives had two 12-cylinder diesel engines and a separate transmission for the drive to each bogie. Class 42 (Maybach/Mekydro) was powered by Maybach MD650 engines. In the first three locomotives the engines were set to give 1,056hp at 1,400rpm but in the remainder of the class the setting was 1,135hp at 1,530rpm. Class 43 (MAN/Voith) had MAN L12V18/21B engines set to 1,100hp at 1,530rpm. One locomotive of Class 43 was powered by two Paxman 12YJX engines also operating at the 1,135hp/1,530rpm setting of the rest of the class.

Multiple-unit control was fitted but it was not possible to operate every locomotive in the class with every other, and in the course of time the equipment was removed. In 1968 it was restored in a number of Class 42 locomotives so that they could double-head trains in an accelerated West of England service, supplementing the fleet of 2,700hp 'Westerns'.

Class 42 locomotives were built at Swindon, and Class 43 at Glasgow by the North British Locomotive Company. All carried warship names except D800, which was named *Sir Brian Robertson* after the Chairman of the British Transport Commission, and D812, named *The Royal Naval Reserve 1859-1959.*

Above:
The first 13 of the D800 'Warships' were originally built with three figure WR headcode brackets and discs as displayed by No D805 *Benbow* leaving Teignmouth with the 07.15 Plymouth-Paddington train on 2 July 1959. The locomotive is in original green livery to which yellow warning panels were later added. *S. Creer*

Left:
Double heading of 'Warships' was a regular feature of certain Western Region expresses in the 1960s. Nos D822 *Hercules* and 869 *Zest* pass Aller Junction in June 1969 with the 15.20 Penzance-Paddington. *Hercules*, the leading locomotive is in blue livery whilst *Zest* retains maroon paintwork with the addition of full yellow ends. *L. Riley*

Class 35 'Hymek'

Number series: D7000-D7100
Engine: Maybach MD870
Cylinders: Sixteen, 7.3in × 7.9in
Rating: 1,740hp at 1,500rpm
Transmission: Stone-Maybach Mekydro 6184U hydraulic transmission
Maximum speed: 90mph

Wheel arrangement: B-B
Driving wheel dia: 3ft 9in
Continuous TE: 33,950lb at 9.5mph
Maximum TE: 49,700lb
Weight: 75ton
First loco built: May 1961
Last loco withdrawn: March 1975

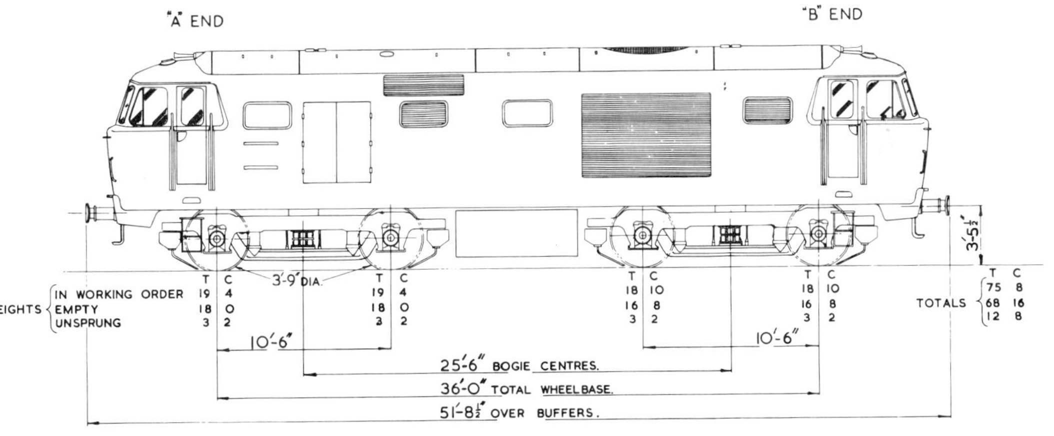

Above:
General arrangement of 1,740hp Class 35 diesel-hydraulic 'Hymek' B-B.

Two new diesel-hydraulic locomotives made their appearance in 1961. First by a few months was the 'Hymek' B-B, powered by one engine of 1,700hp which made it the most powerful single-engined diesel-hydraulic on the Western Region and the only locomotive of that type in the Type 3 power class. The builders were Beyer Peacock & Co Ltd, who had expanded their diesel production capacity with the ending of Beyer-Garratt steam locomotive contracts. Hymeks followed conventional principles of construction in having a separate underframe carrying a body framework supporting plates which did not carry load, in contrast with the stressed skin construction of Classes 42 and 43 where the thin

Below:
The only Type 3 diesel-hydraulic was the Beyer Peacock 'Hymek' Class 35, which differed both in construction and appearance from the other WR hydraulics. In the attractive green livery with yellow warning panels, No D7086 stands at Swindon on 20 September 1964. *B. Stephenson*

plating of the body sides and roof was stress-bearing and contributed to the strength. The Commonwealth bogies, with swing bolsters and primary springs between the equalising beams and the bogie frame, were also in the traditional mould. These were mixed traffic locomotives covering the whole range of WR services. On top-class expresses they ran in the 80s without difficulty when necessary and did not suffer from the stability problems of the more adventurously designed 'Warships' before the Krauss-Maffei bogies were modified. Space inside the locomotive was restricted, and where the passage between the cabs passed one of the radiator banks it was not more than 18in wide. The locomotives had a distinctive convex front end contour and large rectangular louvred openings in the bodysides for air supply to the radiators.

Two new features were the 16-cylinder Maybach MD870 engine (all other engines in the WR main line diesel-hydraulics were 12-cylinder), and the K184 Mekydro transmission, a development of the K104 used in the 'Warships' to take a higher input. The engine had the same piston-swept volume as Maybach's MD865 but was intercooled to increase the rating. In the Hymek locomotives the setting was 1,740hp at 1,500rpm. Pneumatic control gave continuous variation of engine speed instead of the notched control of the previous classes. Two locomotives could work in multiple with one driver and some were operated in this way as bankers on the Lickey Incline. When heavy freights required three helpers, the third Hymek was manned. The locomotives could not run in multiple with other classes.

With only one engine and transmission unit, the layout of the drive was similar to that in the D6300 locomotives but the larger engine and deeper transmission resulted in more steeply-angled cardan shafts. The K184 transmission was in the centre of the locomotive, with an output at each end coupled by cardan shaft to the final drive gearbox on the inner axle of each bogie. Short cardan shafts within each bogie transmitted the drive to corresponding gearboxes on the outer axles.

The class numbered 101 locomotives, all built at the Beyer Peacock Works in six batches, deliveries extending from May 1961 to February 1964.

Class 52 'Western'

Number series: D1000-D1073
Engines: Two Maybach MD655
Cylinders: Twelve, 7.3in × 7.9in
Rating: 1,350hp at 1,500rpm
Transmission: Two Voith-NBL L630rV hydraulic transmissions
Maximum speed: 90mph
Wheel arrangement: C-C
Driving wheel dia: 3ft 7in
Continuous TE: 45,200lb at 14.5mph
Maximum TE: 72,600lb
Weight: 108ton
First loco built: December 1961
Last loco withdrawn: February 1977

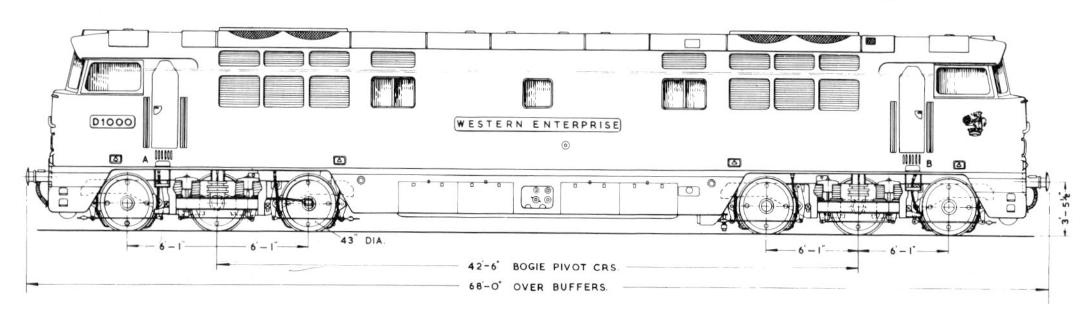

Above:
General arrangement of 2,700hp Class 52 diesel-hydraulic 'Western' C-C. *R. S. Carter*

The second new diesel-hydraulic class of 1961 was the C-C 'Western' (BR Class 52). By the end of the 1950s the Western Region was looking for a more powerful locomotive than the 'Warships' for the accelerated services that were being planned. In West Germany Krauss-Maffei had rebuilt a B-B locomotive as a prototype C-C with a rating of 3,000hp. Its performance was watched with interest by Paddington and led to the decision that the next step for the Western Region should be a six-axle locomotive of similar power.

The German C-C had two Maybach MD655 12-cylinder engines, a version of the MD650 used in the 'Warships' with a rating some 25% higher achieved by intercooling. These were the engines selected for the new Western Region C-C. A licence to build them in Britain had been granted to Bristol Siddeley Engines in 1958. The chosen

Above:
The largest of the diesel hydraulic designs and the last in BR service were the Class 52 'Western' diesels. Here No D1069 *Western Vanguard* leaves Aller Junction behind at the head of the 08.30 Paddington-Penzance on 15 May 1969, carrying the BR blue livery with yellow ends which suited these locomotives well. *W. A. Camwell*

transmission was the Voith L630rV, a higher-capacity design than the Voith unit in the 'Warships'. Its manufacture for the new locomotives was shared between the Voith works in Heidenheim and North British in Glasgow; and later by Voith Engineering (Glasgow) Ltd when North British was going into liquidation.

Mechanical construction of the new locomotives was divided between Swindon and Crewe. The stressed skin body was built on similar principles to the 'Warships' but the bulbous end contours were flattened and the cab front windows made deeper. With a slight overhang above the windows, the roof gave a domestic touch so that one could imagine the cab to be a glazed lean-to conservatory for raising potted plants.

The bogies were a three-axle adaptation of the two-axle Krauss-Maffei design in the 'Warships', retaining the hinged arms housing the outer axleboxes. The axleboxes of the middle axle, however, worked in maganese-faced guides in the bogie frame. The drive from the transmission unit was taken by cardan shaft to a distributor gearbox mounted on the adjacent bogie between the outer and centre axles. Two cardan shafts coupled the gearbox to the final drives on these axles, while a further cardan shaft provided the coupling from the centre to the inner axle. The power handled by the bogie-mounted gearbox made it necessary for it to be water-cooled by a small bleed from the main engine/transmission cooling system.

The diesel engines had continuous pneumatic speed control. Although this was similar to the Hymek system, the 'Western' class was not fitted for multiple operation. All the locomotive names allied 'Western' with some other evocative word, skilfully chosen to give stirring combinations reminiscent of the rich medieval polysyllables of the Southern's 'King Arthurs'. *Western Challenger* and *Western Firebrand* seemed to breathe defiance at Regions of British Railways which had submitted more meekly to their nationalised yoke.

The 'Western' class worked top passenger duties on all WR main lines including Paddington-Birmingham-Birkenhead in the period before electrification from Euston reduced the route to secondary status. They were also seen on freight, particularly stone trains from the Merehead quarries. Wear of cardan shaft splines and seizure of transmission bearings was a problem at one time, leading to a brief withdrawal of the whole class, but the difficulty was overcome by redesign of the system for relieving the cardans of torque reaction stresses.

Class 14

Number series: D9500-D9555
Engine: Paxman Ventura 6YJX
Cylinders: Six
Rating: 650hp at 1,500rpm
Transmission: Voith L217U hydraulic transmission
Maximum speed: 40mph

Wheel arrangement: 0-6-0DH
Driving wheel dia: 4ft 0in
Continuous TE: 26,690lb at 5.6mph
Maximum TE: 30,910lb
Weight: 50ton
First loco built: July 1964
Last loco withdrawn: April 1969

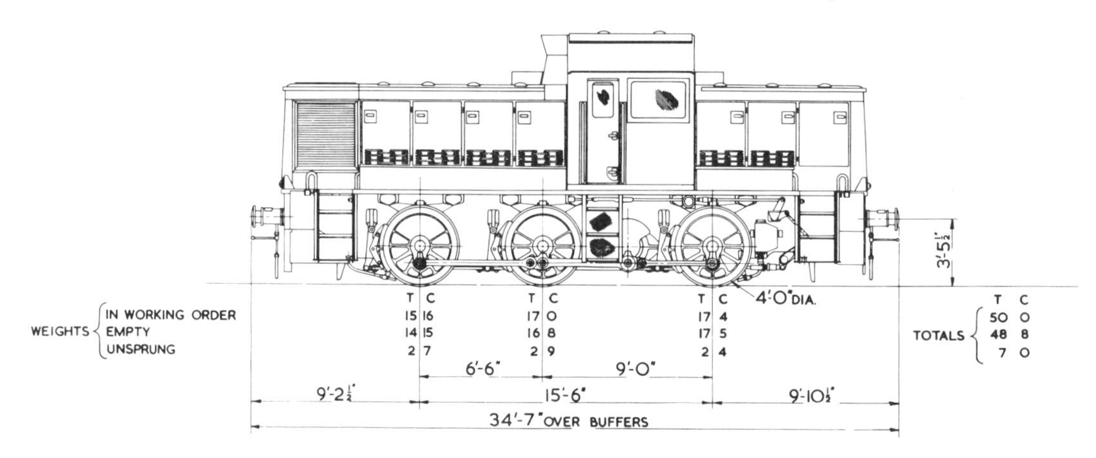

While other Regions used versions of the BR standard 350hp diesel-electric shunter both for shunting and trip working, the Western Region in 1964 introduced its own 650hp diesel-hydraulic design for these duties. The locomotive was a centre-cab 0-6-0 with jackshaft and coupling rod drive and on trip work could run at up to 40mph. A Paxman Ventura 560hp 6-cylinder vee engine was coupled by cardan shaft to a Voith/North British L217/u transmission with two torque converters and a fluid coupling. The torque converters operated in the lower speed range. For full speed the drive was direct through the fluid coupling. The transmission was coupled by a second cardan shaft to a triple-reduction and reverse gearbox with jackshaft output. The reverse gear was pneumatically operated. Fifty-six of these locomotives were built.

Above:
General arrangement of 650hp Class 14 diesel-hydraulic 0-6-0.

Below:
The unusual Class 14 locomotives had absurdly short lives with British Rail, although many were sold for years of further use in industry. No D9521 is seen with the sort of trip working for which they were built passing Acton Main Line.

6 DC Electric Locomotives

Class 70

Number series: 20001-20003†
Rated horsepower: 1,470hp
Equipment: Six E E nose-suspended traction motors
Power supply: 630-750Vdc third rail or overhead
Maximum speed: 75mph
Wheel arrangement: Co-Co
Wheel dia: 3ft 6in
Maximum TE: 40,000lb*
Weight: 99ton 14cwt*
First loco built: 1941
Last loco withdrawn: January 1969

† Nos 20001/2 originally CC1 and CC2
* No 20003 maximum TE 45,000lb, weight 104ton 14cwt

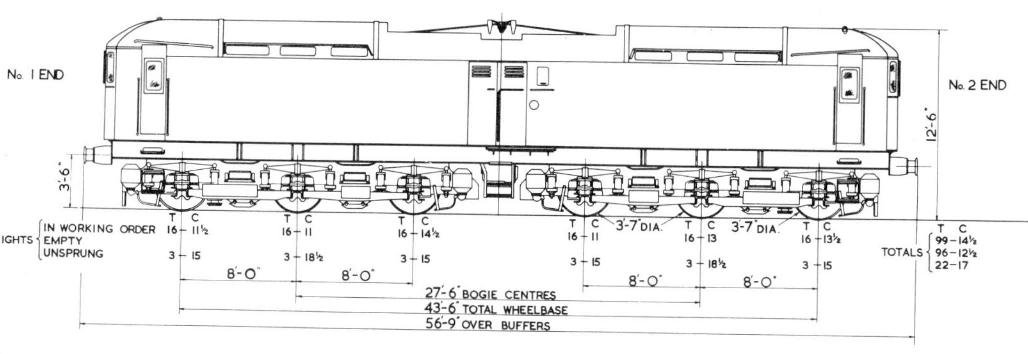

Above:
General arrangement of Southern Region 1,470hp Class 70 electric Co-Co Nos 20001/2.

Below:
General arrangement of Southern Region 1,470hp Class 70 electric Co-Co No 20003.

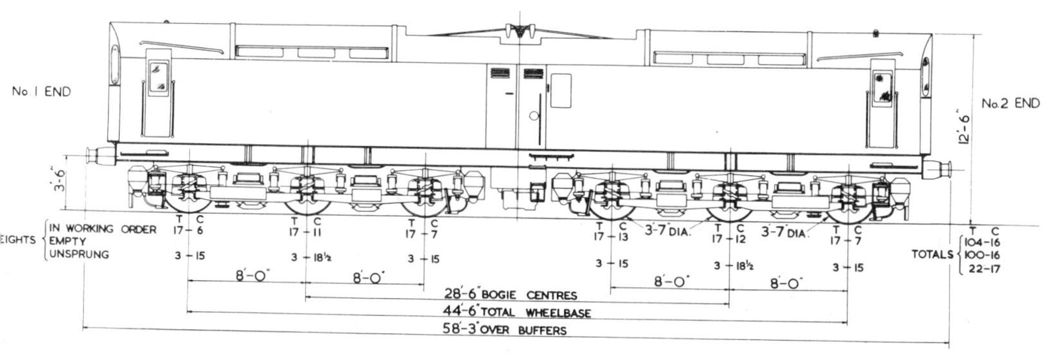

esign of the three Co-Co electric locomotives of e Southern Region, Nos 20001-3, originated with e Southern Railway and the first of them was introduced in 1942. The third of the class did not go into service until 1949. The control system in these locomotives was based on using the output of

Above:
Southern 'booster' Co-Co electric No 20003 approaches Clapham Junction with the down Newhaven boat train on 2 June 1949. *C. C. B. Herbert*

motor-generator (MG) sets first to oppose, and then to supplement the voltage applied to the traction motors from the third rail. During the opposing phase, in which the MG set voltage was progressively reduced, allowing the voltage at the motors to rise correspondingly, the effect was similar to accelerating on resistances but without the energy losses. At zero volts from the MG set, the full live rail voltage was applied to the traction motors. The connections were then reversed and the MG set excited so that generation was resumed, but now an increasing voltage was added to that from the live rail until at full excitation the voltage across each circuit of three traction motors in series was 1,200V, or 400V per motor.

With this system all controller notches could be used continuously. There were 26, including three weak-field steps, as compared with 10 continuous running notches in the contemporary Bo+Bo design of locomotive for the Manchester-Sheffield-Wath electrification. Equally important in a third rail locomotive was the fact that a flywheel weighing 1ton on each motor-generator shaft kept the machines running when the supply was interrupted at gaps, maintaining an input to the traction motors until the collector shoes were again in contact with the live rail. The locomotives carried a pantograph for use in yards and sidings where overhead wiring had been installed.

Another feature of the locomotives was the Bulleid design of bogie, with the body carried directly on the bogie frames in two bearings forming opposite segments of a circle of 9ft diameter. The segmental bearings allowed rotational movements of the bogies on curves and by their wide spacing minimised the tendency to weight transfer between axles caused by the bogies tilting when starting with high tractive efforts. Similar bogies, but with an additional carrying axle, were adopted for the Southern's diesel-electrics and by British Railways for diesel-electric locomotives of Classes 40, 44, 45 and 46. The Southern Co-Cos worked the first locomotive-hauled express electric passenger service in Britain, being allotted, among their other duties, to the Victoria-Newhaven boat trains. No 20003 took the first locomotive-hauled electric Newhaven boat train out of Victoria on 1 May 1949.

Classes 71 and 74

Number series: E5001-E5024†
Rated horsepower: 2,552hp
Equipment: Four EE spring-borne traction motors
Power supply: 630-750Vdc
Maximum speed: 90mph
Wheel arrangement: Bo-Bo
Wheel dia: 4ft 0in
Maximum TE: 43,800lb
Weight: 77ton
First loco built: February 1959
Last loco withdrawn: November 1977

† Later E5001-E5014 only. Renumbered 71.001-71.014

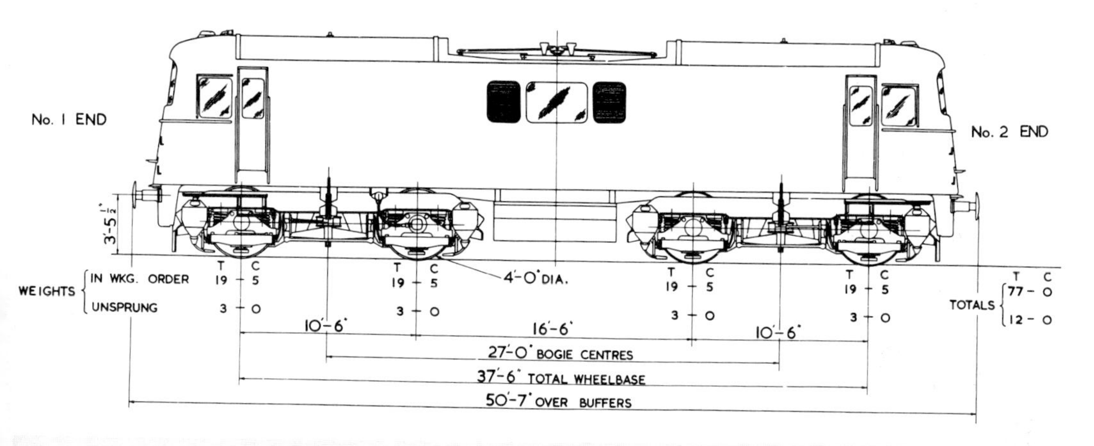

Top:
General arrangement of 2,552hp Class 71 electric Bo-Bo.

Above:
Carrying all green body livery with red buffer beams, ex-works Class 71 No E5005 built by BR at Doncaster stands at Eastleigh on 27 May 1963. The pantograph for working on sections with overhead wires instead of the third rail can be seen in the centre of the roof. *R. A. Panting*

In 1959 the Southern Region extended its 750V dc electrification from Gillingham to Dover via Canterbury, and along the North Kent coast to Ramsgate. Most of the passenger traffic, including boat trains, was worked by EMUs but two of the Continental services needed locomotive haulage. These were the Pullman 'Golden Arrow', and the 'Night Ferry' with its Wagon-Lits sleeping cars which crossed the Channel on the Dover-Dunkerque train ferry, providing a through service between London and Paris. For working these trains and also for freight traffic, 15 Bo-Bo locomotives of 2,500hp were built, forming Class 71.

The booster principle of Nos 20001-3 was retained but with changes based on experience with the earlier design. Instead of two booster sets, each connected to three motors, one set now served the four motors. Cooling air for the motors was supplied by a separate motor-blower set, instead of from blowers on the booster set shafts, but the auxiliary supply, which in the Co-Co class had come from a separate motor-generator, was now provided by an auxiliary generator overhung on the shaft of the booster set. A new type of controller, soon to become familiar in the LMR electric locomotives, was adopted. It allowed the driver to notch up step by step, or to leave the equipment to run through the notches automatically, with the ability to stop it on any notch by returning the handle to a 'hold' position. There were 33 notches.

In mechanical design the locomotives reflected developments which had been taking place on the Continent in Bo-Bo classes for fast passenger work. The traction motors were fully springborne, with spring drives, and were mounted in bogies based on a Swiss design in which rubber-bushed joints and other rubber components reduced the number of points where friction could produce wear. A pantograph for use in sidings with overhead wiring was fitted as in the earlier locomotives. The locomotive weight of 77 tons was in striking contrast with the 104 tons of the third of the 1,470hp Co-Co series.

When electrification to Bournemouth was nearing completion the Southern Region reconsidered its locomotive requirements. The Bournemouth line would need locomotives capable of working heavy trains at speeds up to the line limit of 90mph, with an accelerating power that would match that of the EMUs. Provision for working through sections where power was cut off for maintenance, and on non-electrified lines, was also necessary. This meant a more powerful version of the electro-diesels, the first of which had been introduced in 1962. It was decided that ten of the Class 71 electric locomotives should be converted into 2,550hp electro-diesels to meet this specification.

Number series: E6101-E6110†
Engine: Paxman 6YJXL
Cylinders: Six
Rating: 650hp at 1,500rpm
Electric power rating: 2,552hp
Equipment: Four EE spring-borne traction motors
Maximum speed: 90mph

Wheel arrangement: Bo-Bo
Wheel dia: 4ft 0in
Continuous TE: diesel: 18,100lb
Maximum TE: diesel: 40,000lb
electric: 47,500lb
Weight: 85ton
First loco built: November 1967*
Last loco withdrawn: December 1977

† Later renumbered 74.001-74.010
* Rebuilt from Class 71, introduced 1959

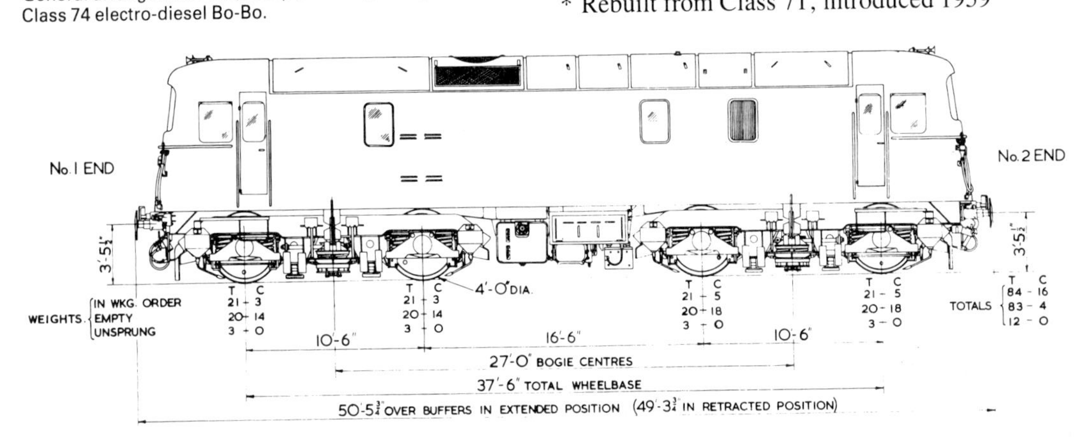

Below:
General arrangement of 2,552hp (electric), 650hp (diesel) Class 74 electro-diesel Bo-Bo.

The converted locomotives were designated Class 74. A booster control system was retained, but without the flywheels, for it had been found that the inertia of the armatures kept the machines running and supplying sufficient power to avoid snatching at couplings or discomfort to passengers when power from the live rail was abruptly cut off and then restored at conductor rail gaps. A 650hp diesel engine and generator provided the input to the booster set when the locomotive was working off the live rail so that the control was the same whether running on electric or diesel power. The controller had four main running notches and one shunting notch, for it was found that four characteristics would meet operating requirements. On all running notches the generator excitation wa under continuous electronic control, givin 'stepless' increase of motor voltage to maintain steady current until the machines were operating o the selected tractive effort/speed curve. This was a early application of electronic control with soli state devices and encountered various problems including some unforeseen difficulties in securin printed circuit boards in racks when subject t vibration in a locomotive at speed.

Class 74 was designed to fit in with th Bournemouth line operating principle o interchangeable motive power and could work i

multiple with EMUs, Class 33 diesel-electrics, or other electro-diesels, and could be controlled from a remote driving cab (although the shunting notch was not then available). Its four running characteristics corresponded to those of the four-notch controller standardised throughout the Southern Region's fleet. Working Southampton boat trains had been an important activity but as regular liner services were withdrawn the locomotives were less in demand. Withdrawals began in 1976.

Above:
The former No E5005 is seen near the end of its life having been rebuilt as a Class 74 electro-diesel. No 74.008 ascends the bank out of Poole with an Eastleigh-bound parcels train on 5 April 1977. *L. A. Nixon*

Class 73

Number series: E6001-E6049†
Engine: English Electric 4SRKT MkII
Cylinders: Four
Rating: 600hp at 850rpm
Electric power rating: 1,600hp
Equipment: Four E E axle-suspended traction motors
Maximum speed: 90mph

Wheel arrangement: Bo-Bo
Wheel dia: 3ft 4in
Continuous TE: diesel: 13,600lb at 11.5mph
Maximum TE: diesel: 36,000lb
electric: 40,000lb
Weight: 75ton 12cwt
First loco built: 1962; 73/1 1965

† Later renumbered 73.001-73.006 and 73.101-73.142

Note: Above details apply to E6007-E6049, Class 73/1

E6001-E6006 Class 73/0
Maximum speed: 80mph
Electric power rating: 1,600hp

Continuous TE: diesel: 16,000lb at 10mph
Maximum TE: diesel: 34,000lb
electric: 42,000lb
Weight: 75ton 2cwt

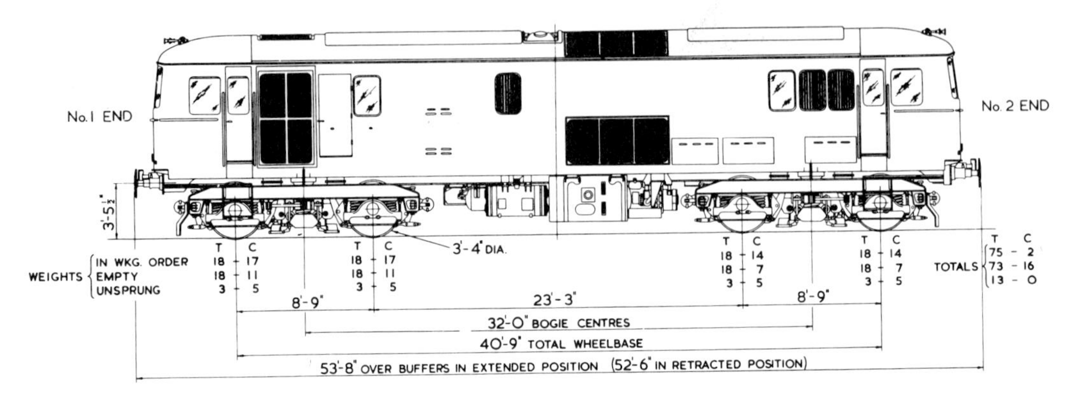

Above:
General arrangement of 1,600hp (electric), 600hp (diesel) Class 73 electro-diesel Bo-Bo.

From the early days of Southern Railway main line electrification it had been foreseen that as the steam locomotive fleet was reduced, it would be necessary to have some form of motive power capable of operating over sections where no live rail supply was available. A first step in this direction was taken when electrification reached Dover via Canterbury in 1959 and 'motorised' luggage vans were built for running in Continental boat trains. The vans carried batteries which powered the motors when operating on non-electrified quayside lines at the ports. Battery power was limited, however, and although the vans were self-propelled they could not haul a heavy load. A more versatile unit was needed and the answer was an electric locomotive with auxiliary diesel power for use where there was no live rail, or where the live rail was 'dead' for maintenance or other reasons. This hybrid was called an 'electro-diesel'. It was not feasible to instal a diesel engine equivalent in power to the electric traction equipment but on diesel power the locomotive could haul heavy loads in a lower speed range, or two could work in multiple.

The first of six Class 73/0 electro-diesels appeared in 1962. This is a Bo-Bo electric locomotive with conventional resistance and series/parallel control, and a rating on electric power of 1,600hp. Also inside the locomotive body is a diesel engine with a rating of 600hp at 800rpm, coupled to an electric generator for supplying the traction motors when no live rail supply is available. On diesel power a normal diesel-electric control system comes into action, although with a feature unusual in British practice, in that series/parallel switching of the traction motors takes place as during electric working, initiated in this case by the load regulator.

On electric power the driver can notch up by

Below:
Class 73/0 electro-diesel No 73.004 passes East Croydon on a London Bridge-Brighton working on 7 September 1979. The extra jumper cables cater for two auxiliary system voltages. *J. Scrace*

hand or allow the equipment to run up automatically to weak-field in series or in parallel. A 'hold' position on the controller enables him to stop the automatic notching at any point. Although there may then be some resistance in circuit, the resistances have highly efficient natural ventilation and can carry a current of 950A continuously at a temperature of 600°C. For changing to diesel power, which can be done while the locomotive is running, the electric power handle is returned to a 'lock-off' position, which releases the diesel power handle below it. The collector shoes are lifted automatically, and the locomotive is controlled by varying the diesel engine speed in the usual way.

The 42 generally similar locomotives of Class 73/1 followed in 1965. They were geared for 90mph (Class 73/0 has 80mph gears). In both classes the diesel engine is started by operating a single switch but in Class 73/1 it can be started similarly from a remote driving cab. Air for the traction motor blowers in Class 73/0 was drawn from inside the locomotive body. It was found that this arrangement caused draughts in the cab, and in Class 73/1 the air is drawn from outside through filters. Class 73/0 locomotives have been modified similarly. Both classes were designed for operating in multiple with each other, with Class 33 diesels, and with EMU stock. When Class 73/0 locomotives were built they were fitted with duplicate control jumper receptacles to cater for 70V or 110V control systems. By the time the 73/1 locomotives came into service, relays which could operate in the 70-110V range without their coils overheating had been introduced and in conjunction with other control system developments made duplication unnecessary.

Some EMU cabs are equipped for changing an electro-diesel in the same train from electric to diesel working. When this is done, the standard four-position EMU controller selects four different engine speeds by coded electric signals to the pneumatic system acting on the engine governor. With direct control from the electro-diesel cab, however, the engine speed is continuously variable.

Class 76 (EM1)*

Number series: E26000-E26057†
Rated horsepower: 1,868hp
Equipment: Four Metropolitan-Vickers nose-suspended traction motors
Power supply: 1,500Vdc overhead
Maximum speed: 65mph

Wheel arrangement: Bo+Bo
Wheel dia: 4ft 2in
Maximum TE: 45,000lb
Weight: 87ton 15cwt
First loco built: March 1950*
Last loco withdrawn: July 1981

† Later renumbered 76.001-76.057
* Refers to 26001 of production build. Prototype 26000 built 1941

Below:
General arrangement of 1,868hp Class 76 electric Bo+Bo.

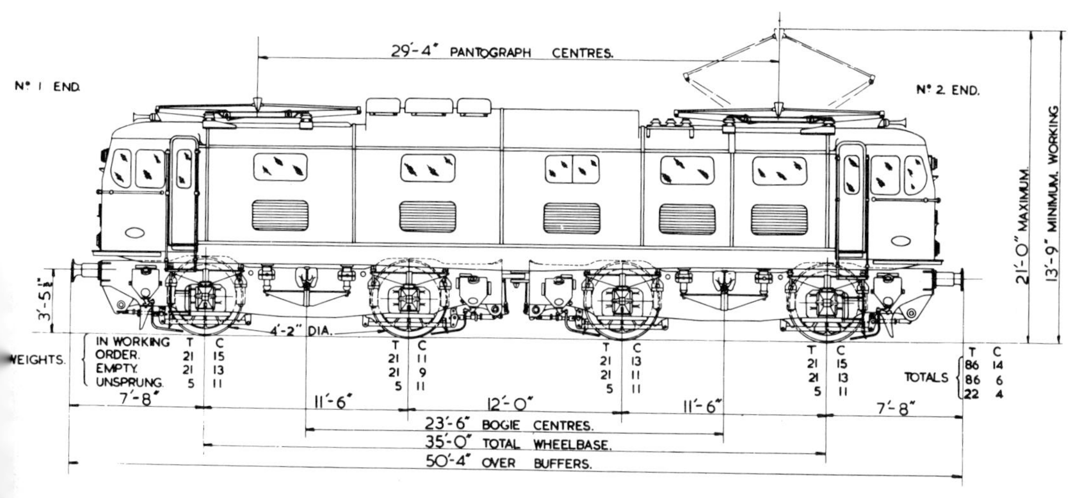

* The first locomotive of the type that formed BR Class 76 was built in 1941 and carried the LNER number 6701, later becoming No 6000. At the end of World War 2 it was sent on loan to the Netherlands Railways, acquiring the name *Tommy*, which was carried officially after its return to this country. The locomotive was renumbered 26000 by BR and withdrawn in March 1970.

Above:
A pair of Class 76 1,500V dc electrics passes Huddersfield Junction, Penistone, with coal for Wigan power station on 31 May 1974. No 76.015 leads 76.022. These locomotives were withdrawn when the Woodhead route's non-standard electrical equipment became due for replacement, operations finishing in 1981. *F. R. Kerr*

Class 76 represented the classic dc locomotive with resistance control. The design originated before World War 2 in the early stages of planning electrification at 1,500V dc of the former Great Central main line from Sheffield to Manchester via the Woodhead Tunnel, together with the branch from Penistone to the marshalling yards at Wath. Wheel arrangement was Bo+Bo, the plus sign indicating that the bogies were coupled together and carried the buffing and drawgear so that the tractive and braking forces were borne by them. The four traction motors were axle-hung but rubber elements between the toothed rim and the hub of the gearwheels gave some resilience in the drive. Gradients on the route across the Pennines were long and severe and the locomotives were equipped for regenerative braking so that trains descending the banks could return power to the overhead line. When this 'bonus' power could not be absorbed by other trains, the regenerated current was switched automatically into resistances at certain substations. From 1959 the locomotives were modified so that rheostatic braking was also available, enabling the range over which the locomotives could be braked electrically to be extended from 16-18mph down to 3 or 4mph.

Control was entirely manual, the driver having separate levers for notching, changing the motor grouping and controlling regeneration. With four weak-field steps and two motor groupings, the locomotives had ten economic running speeds. By transmitting tractive effort at low level, the tendency to weight transfer between axles when starting heavy trains was reduced, but as a further precaution the tractive effort of the motors driving the leading bogie axles could be restricted by closing a weight transfer switch which weakened their fields.

Class 76 proved a highly reliable mixed traffic locomotive and periods between maintenance were actually extended in the closing years of the electrification. After Manchester-Sheffield passenger traffic by the Woodhead route was withdrawn on 1 January 1970 they continued working heavy freight, and in the late 1960s larger compressors for handling air-braked trains were installed in 21 locomotives which had not been equipped with train-heating boilers. At the same time they were converted for working in multiple in pairs. A further nine were given larger compressors and multiple equipment in 1974 and on this occasion the vacuum braking gear was removed. The 'end of the line' for the class came when the Woodhead route was closed except for the Manchester-Hadfield/Glossop and Sheffield-Penistone sections as from 18 July 1981. Two years later the Sheffield-Penistone service was diverted via Barnsley.

Class 77 (EM2)

Number series: E27000-E27006
Rated horsepower: 2,490hp
Equipment: Six Metropolitan-Vickers nose-suspended traction motors
Power supply: 1,500Vdc overhead
Maximum speed: 90mph
Wheel arrangement: Co-Co
Wheel dia: 3ft 7in
Maximum TE: 45,000lb
Weight: 102ton 10cwt
First loco built: December 1953
Last loco withdrawn: September 1968

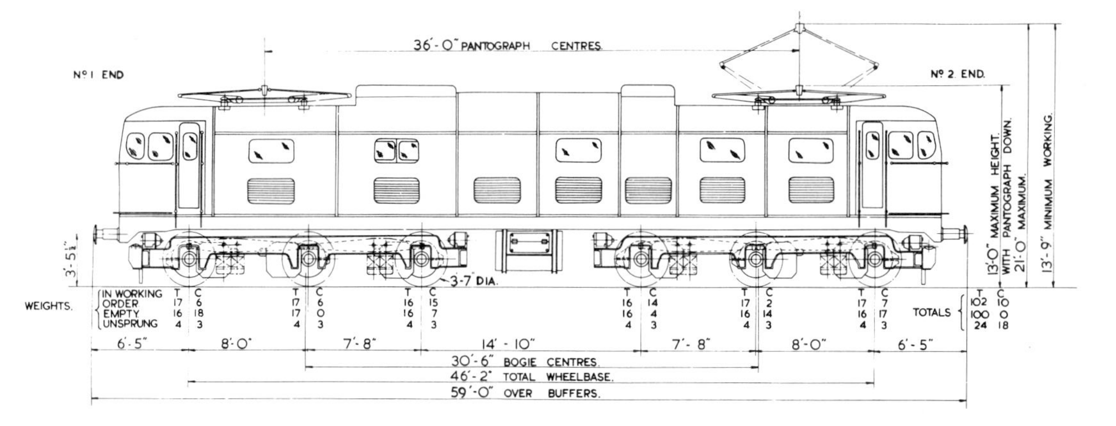

Above:
General arrangement of 2,490hp Class 77 electric Co-Co.

Below:
The first of seven 'EM2', TOPS Class 77, locomotives No 27000, later named *Electra* leads a mixed rake of stock on one of its first runs. All seven members of the class were sold to Netherlands State Railways after withdrawal by British Rail. *BR (LM)*

When the Manchester-Sheffield 1,500V dc electrification went into full passenger and freight operation on 14 September 1954, the Class 76 mixed traffic locomotives which had been working freight for two years were joined by the seven Co-Co express passenger locomotives of Class 77. This was a postwar design but still in the conventional dc tradition. With six traction motors, three motor groupings were available and came into effect in sequence automatically as the power handle was moved round its quadrant. Three weak-field steps could be used in each grouping. They were selected by the regeneration handle as an addition to its main function of controlling braking effort, which was not required while motoring. There was no weight-transfer switch but if slipping occurred the driver notched back and pressed an anti-slip brake pedal which made a partial brake application on all axles.

Buffers and drawgear were on the main frame and there was no inter-bogie coupling. The motors were axle-hung although maximum service speed was 90mph. There was considerable resistance to flexible drives at that period although in Continental practice they were general for speeds of that order. It was recognised, however, that lateral movements of the heavy motors could increase the stresses on the track at high speeds and in these locomotives they were restrained by struts with rubber-bushed attachments to the motor and bogie frames. All the class were equipped with train-heating boilers.

The decline of passenger service on the Woodhead route, particularly withdrawal of the Manchester-Marylebone expresses eventually made the Class 77 locomotives redundant, although a regular-interval timetable of fast passenger trains between Manchester and Sheffield was operated up to the end of 1969. In 1971 the seven locomotives were sold to the Netherlands Railways.

7 AC Electric Locomotives

When British Railways decided to adopt high-voltage ac electrification at 50Hz in the mid-1950s the 50Hz traction motor was already giving way on the Continent to dc motors fed through rectifiers. BR used rectifiers from the outset, beginning with EMUs on the Lancaster-Morecambe-Heysham trial section and then in 1959 on the Colchester-Clacton-Walton pilot scheme in the Eastern Region. The first of BR's electric locomotives were built for the London Midland Region's electrification from Manchester and Liverpool to Stoke-on-Trent, Birmingham and Euston. There were five prototype classes, all of Bo-Bo wheel arrangement and conforming to a common performance specification but varying in details of their mechanical construction and electrical equipment. Originally designated AL1 to AL5, the prototypes were reclassified as Classes 81 to 85 under the renumbering system of 1973.

While manufacturers were free to develop their own ideas in many respects certain components had to be used by them all because at the time there were no British equivalents already proved in service. These were air-blast circuit-breakers, pantographs and flexible drives. The air-blast circuit-breakers in the first locomotives came from Brown-Boveri, but a similar pattern developed in Britain by Associated Electrical Industries (AEI) was installed in some later locomotives and EMUs for comparative trials. Pantographs were a modification of the Faiveley 'single-arm' type used on ac locomotives of the French National Railways, made under licence in this country by J. Stone & Co (Deptford) Ltd. These pantographs were fitted on 99 of the 100 prototype locomotives. The exception was No E3055 of Class 82 which had AEI 'crossed-arm' pantographs of the type seen later on certain Class 86 locomotives and throughout Class 87. Two pantographs were carried by all locomotives at first but one was later removed.

Two types of flexible drive were specified. One was the Alsthom drive with rubber-bushed links connecting drive arms on a quill shaft to opposite corners of a 'floating ring', the other corners of which were similarly connected to the driving wheel. The second was a Brown-Boveri/SLM drive in which torque was transmitted by spring-loaded pads within the main gearwheel to the arms of a 'star' wheel mounted on the axle. These arrangements enabled the traction motors to be wholly supported by the bogie frames instead of half their weight being carried by the axle as in the axle-hung arrangement. The flexibility of the springs, or of the combination of rubber-bushed links and floating ring, allowed for movements of the axle with the primary suspension while the centre-to-centre distance of the motor pinion and final gearwheel remained constant.

In Classes 81, 83 and 85 the axleboxes were connected to the bogie frame by rubber-bushed radius arms or links. In Classes 82 and 84 they worked between fixed guides. Class 82 was the only one of the prototype classes with the bogie frame produced as a one-piece casting.

All locomotives had tap-changer control but this took two forms. In Classes AL2 and AL4 the tappings were on the winding of a high-tension auto-transformer, and a variable voltage was applied to a fixed-ratio transformer with its secondary connected to the rectifiers. In Classes AL1, AL3 and AL5 the tap-changer operated on the low-tension secondary of a two-winding transformer.

Driver's controls in all classes were of a standard form, which has been continued in the later Classes 86 and 87. The driver can notch up or back one step at a time by moving the power handle to and fro or he can set the handle at a 'run up' or a 'run back' position in which the equipment operates automatically until stopped by placing the handle at 'hold'. Another feature carried through from the prototypes is automatic power control (APC) for opening the circuit-breaker on approaching a neutral (non-energised) section of the overhead system and re-closing it on reaching the 'live' contact wire beyond. The system is triggered by permanent magnets on the track similar to those of the automatic warning system (AWS).

Classes AL1 to AL5 were equipped for operation on 25kV or 6.25kV, with automatic changeover of the transformer connections when passing from one voltage to the other. During electrification of the

LMR lines, however, it was found that 25kV could be used safely where clearances were below the limits originally set and the lower voltage was not used. The dual-voltage switching and sensing arrangements in the locomotives have therefore been disconnected.

Main contractors for the prototype locomotives were Associated Electrical Industries Ltd (AEI) with works at Rugby and Manchester; the English Electric group of companies; and the General Electric Co Ltd, with which the North British Locomotive Co Ltd was associated for manufacture of mechanical parts. Individual characteristics of the prototype and subsequent ac locomotive classes are summarised below (original class numbers in brackets). The contractors named above are now merged into GEC Traction Ltd.

Class 81 (AL1)

Number series: E3001-E3023, E3096, E3097†
Rated horsepower: 3,200hp
Equipment: Four AEI spring-borne dc traction motors
Power supply: 25kVac overhead
Maximum speed: 100mph

Wheel arrangement: Bo-Bo
Wheel diameter: 4ft 0in
Maximum TE: 50,000lb
Weight: 78ton 3cwt
First loco built: November 1959

† Later renumbered as 81.001-81.022

Below:
General arrangement of 3,200hp Class 81 electric Bo-Bo.

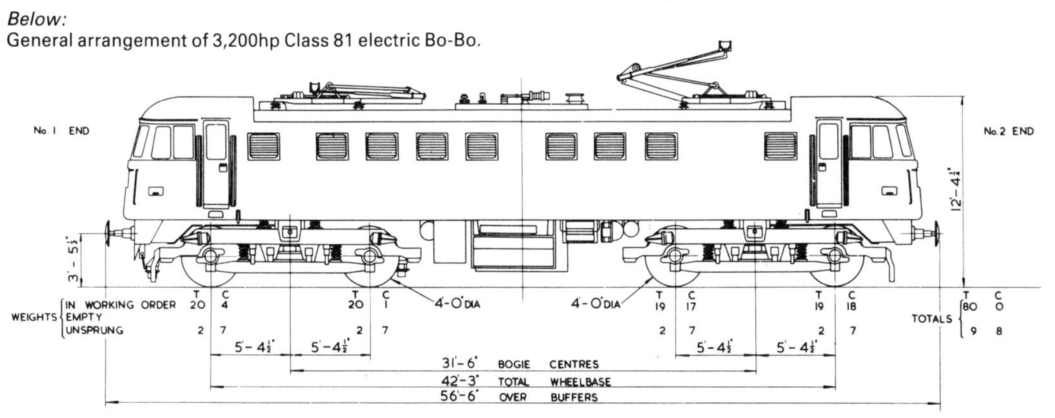

Below:
No 81.017, photographed at Springs Branch on 26 May 1977, belongs to the first of the prototype ac classes ordered for the LMR electrification. The locomotive is in standard blue livery with TOPS numbering and it carries a cast alloy double arrow symbol. *E. Bullen*

The 25 locomotives of this class were supplied by AEI (Rugby), builder of the electrical equipment. Mechanical parts were built by the Birmingham Railway Carriage & Wagon Co Ltd. No 3001 was handed over to BR on 27 November 1959. It had been intended originally that 95 of the 100 prototype locomotives ordered should be geared for 100mph, while the other five would be given a different gear ratio to provide a higher drawbar pull at 55mph for working heavy fully-braked freight trains. The programme of equipping all wagons with power brakes was not pursued as quickly as had been expected, however, and the class was delivered with the 100mph gearing.

The AL1 locomotives had low-tension tap-changer control and three 6-anode mercury-arc rectifiers of an established industrial design but modified to minimise splashing of the mercury pool under vibration. The bogies had fixed bolsters, the pivoting system allowing the relative lateral movements between bogie and body normally provided by swing links. This arrangement was based on Alsthom principles, the pivot consisting of a vertical column with conical rubber bearings in the underframe and the bolster, the rubber allowing both lateral movements, controlled by springs, and rotational movement of the bogie on curves. Tractive effort was transmitted through the rubber, longitudinal stability of the column being maintained by manganese pads. Part of the body weight was carried by side bearers. The flexible drive was by Alsthom rubber-bushed links.

Class 82 (AL2)

Number series: E3046-E3055†
Rated horsepower: 3,300hp
Equipment: Four AEI fully suspended traction motors
Power supply: 25kVac overhead
Maximum speed: 100mph

Wheel arrangement: Bo-Bo
Wheel diameter: 4ft 0in
Maximum TE: 50,000lb
Weight: 78ton 10cwt
First loco built: May 1960
Last loco withdrawn:

† Later renumbered as 82.001-82.008

Below:
General arrangement of 3,300hp Class 82 electric Bo-Bo.

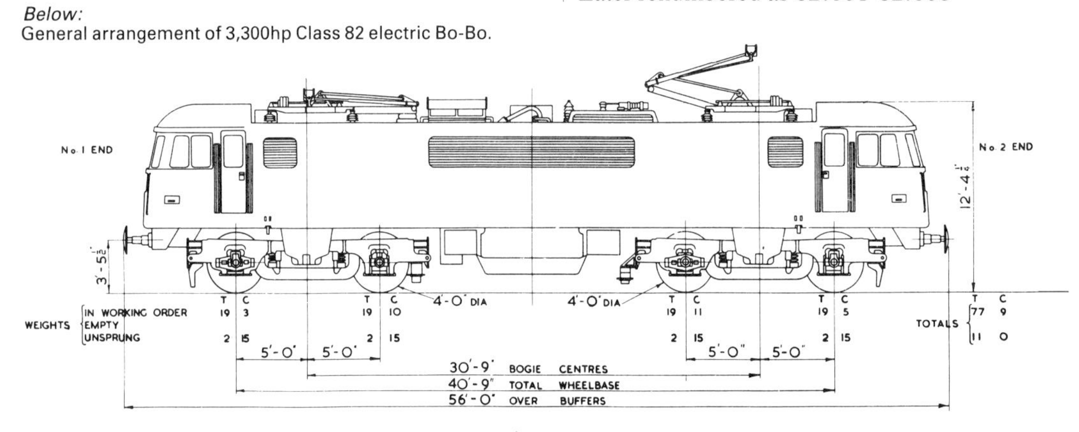

The 10 locomotives of Class 82 were supplied by AEI (Manchester) and the mechanical parts were built by Beyer Peacock & Co Ltd. Rectifiers were similar to Class 81 but control was by a chain-driven high-tension tap-changer. The bogies were a development of those in the gas turbine locomotive built by Metropolitan-Vickers for the Western Region (page 40), the body being carried by links suspended from the bogie frame, their lower ends engaging with body support struts extending downward from the body underframe and passing outside the bogie frame. Both ends of the links carried resilient rubber joints. The upper joints were recessed into a transverse member of the bogie supported on coil springs. This assembly provided all the freedoms of a conventional swing bolster without metallic surfaces subject to wear. Tractive effort was transmitted through the pivots from axle level, the pivot pins being located in bushes in transverse draw-buff beams connecting each pair of body support struts at their lower ends. A rubber-bushed linkage between the bush and the beam allowed lateral movement of 1.75in each way. The flexible drive from the traction motors to the axles was of the Alsthom type described earlier.

Above:
A dramatic action shot of 'AL2', later Class 82, locomotive No E3053 at speed with 09.50 Birmingham-Euston at Sudbury Junction in the early years of the London Midland electrification. The locomotive is in original electric blue livery with yellow end panels. *BR (LM)*

Class 83 (AL3)

Number series: E3024-E3035, E3303, E3304, E3100†
Rated horsepower: 2,950hp
Equipment: Four EE spring-borne dc traction motors
Power supply: 25kVac overhead
Maximum speed: 100mph
Wheel arrangement: Bo-Bo
Wheel diameter: 4ft 0in
Maximum TE: 38,000lb
Weight: 75ton 4cwt
First loco built: July 1960
Last loco withdrawn:

† E3303 and E3304 later E3098/9. Class renumbered as 83.001-83.015

Below:
General arrangement of 2,950hp Class 83 electric Bo-Bo.

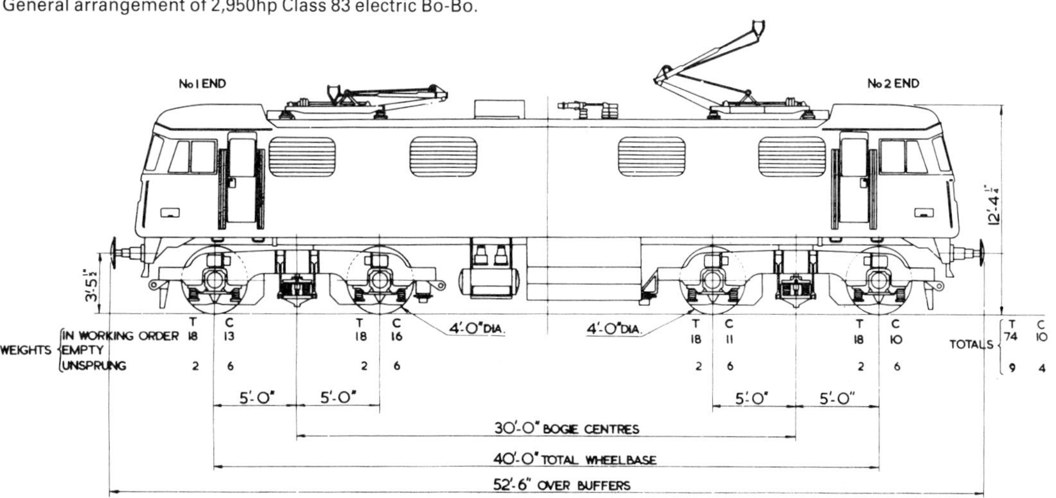

In a multi-anode rectifier of the type used in Classes 81 and 82, a failure would make the whole rectifier unserviceable and involve removal and replacement of a bulky item of equipment. There were advantages for traction in using groups of single-anode rectifiers which were easier to handle and could be replaced individually in case of failure. The problem was that in a single-anode rectifier, the arc would normally be extinguished during the half-cycle when the rectifier was not conducting. In the excitron single-anode rectifier the arc was maintained by diverting it to an

Above:
The last of the 'AL3' class was numbered E3100 and equipped with a transductor control system providing notchless acceleration. This view shows the locomotive in original condition with cast 'lion and wheel' totem.
J. Duncan

auxiliary anode while the main anode was negative to cathode. In the ignitron the arc was re-struck at the beginning of each positive half-cycle. The rectifiers in Class 83 were ignitrons.

Fifteen Class 83 locomotives were supplied by the English Electric Co Ltd and built within the EE Group, the mechanical parts being produced by the company's Vulcan Foundry. All except No 3100 had ignitron rectifiers and low-tension tap-changing with air-motor drive of the camshafts. No 3100 was fitted with silicon rectifiers and a transductor control system acting in conjunction with the tap-changer and avoiding the sudden increase in voltage from one tap to the next. Instead the voltage rose smoothly to that of the higher tapping and the risk of wheelslip was reduced.

Nos 3303-5 in the original numbering of the class were to have been freight ratio locomotives but during the construction period it was decided that No 3305 should be used for the transductor experiments and geared for 100mph. It was renumbered 3100, Nos 3303-4 were built with the freight ratio but converted later and renumbered 3098/99.

Test running with No 3100 provided valuable experience for the development of wheelslip protection, automatic control of tractive effort, and rheostatic braking. In 1962 it was decided to continue experiments with the locomotive geared for 80mph maximum speed and it exchanged bogies with No 3304, the only remaining locomotive with freight-ratio gearing. This was the occasion for the renumbering of 3304 as 3099. No 3100 continued in service with its new bogies and performed to the satisfaction of BR and of the English Electric Company. Events were catching up with it, however, for notchless control with thyristors was becoming practicable, providing continuous voltage control without a tap-changer, and other advantages. The locomotive went into store in 1968 but in 1971 emerged as a standard Class 83 with 100mph gearing. At that period all the 83s were being equipped with silicon rectifiers in place of their original ignitrons.

Class 83 was the only one of the prototypes with three-phase motors for auxiliary drives. The three-phase supply was provided by a rotary converter which also drove a dc generator for battery-charging and the dc drives of the compressors and exhausters. Oil and water pumps, fans and blowers were all on the three-phase system.

Bogie design incorporated a modified design of swing bolster which saved weight. Tractive and braking forces were transmitted to the bolster by rubber-bushed rods so that there were no rubbing metallic surfaces. Brown-Boveri/SLM flexible drives transmitted the motor torque.

Class 84 (AL4)

Number series: E3036-E3045†
Rated horsepower: 3,100hp
Equipment: Four GEC spring-borne dc traction motors
Power supply: 25kVac overhead
Maximum speed: 100mph
Wheel arrangement: Bo-Bo
Wheel diameter: 4ft 0in
Maximum TE: 50,000lb
Weight: 75ton 7cwt
First loco built: March 1960
Last loco withdrawn: November 1980

† Later renumbered as 84.001-84.010

Below:
General arrangement of 3,100hp Class 84 electric Bo-Bo.

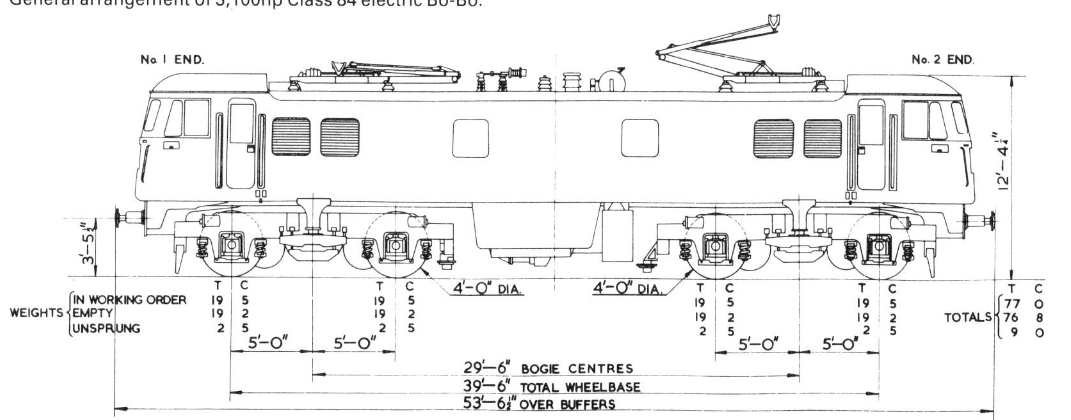

Above:
The NBL-built Class 84 (originally 'AL4') was the first of the prototype classes to be withdrawn completely. No 84.003 is seen in latter-day condition at Crewe in October 1973.
N. E. Preedy

Production of the 10 locomotives of Class 84 was shared between the General Electric Co Ltd as main contractor and supplier of the electrical equipment, and the North British Locomotive Co Ltd as builder of the mechanical parts. For these locomotives GEC had developed a single-anode rectifier called the 'Com-Pak' which was basically an excitron but aimed at providing the best features of the excitron and the ignitron. Control was by tap-changing on a high-tension auto-transformer by means of cam-operated selector switches. The camshaft was motor-driven and was held in the various notch positions by air-operated pawls engaging with two star wheels. This type of tap-changer was not repeated in the post-prototype classes, in which a developed version of the equipment used in Class 82 was installed.

Class 84 bogies were of conventional swing bolster construction but with traction and braking forces transmitted between the bogie frame and bolster by rubber-bushed links. Brown-Boveri/SLM spring drives were fitted.

Class 85 (AL5)

Number series: E3056-E3095†
Rated horsepower: 3,200hp
Equipment: Four AEI fully suspended dc traction motors
Power supply: 25kVac overhead
Maximum speed: 100mph

Wheel arrangement: Bo-Bo
Wheel diameter: 4ft 0in
Maximum TE: 50,000lb
Weight: 81ton 3cwt
First loco built: September 1960

† Later renumbered as 85.001-85.040

Below:
General arrangement of 3,200hp Class 85 electric Bo-Bo.

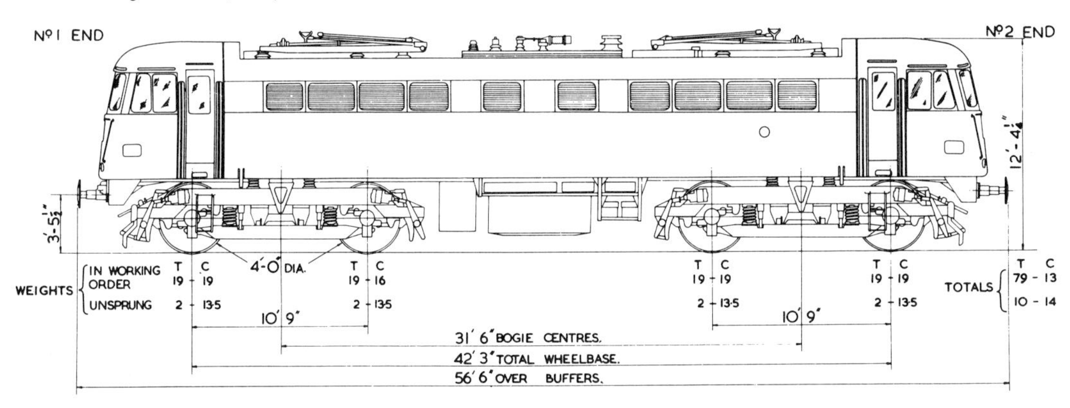

Germanium semiconductor rectifiers were fitted to the EMUs built for the initial Manchester-Crewe and Liverpool-Crewe stages of the LMR electrification and were in operation from 1960. The first BR locomotives with semiconductor

Below:
Semiconductor rectifiers replaced mercury-arcs in the 'AL5', the first BR locomotive to be so equipped, although semiconductors were already in use in EMUs. The motorail train passing Stafford with No 85.040 on 16 August 1978 includes a Pullman marshalled five coaches behind the engine. *A. Swift*

rectifiers were the 40 units of the AL5 prototype class, the first of which went into service in June 1961. They were built by BR at Doncaster. Electrical equipment was supplied by AEI (Rugby) and was basically similar to that of Class 82 but with modifications due to the rectifiers and to the use of rheostatic braking. A preliminary study of the design showed a saving in weight and space compared with earlier designs and it was decided to take advantage of this by installing the rheostatic equipment. As built, Nos 3056 to 3085 had germanium rectifiers, and Nos 3086 to 3095 had silicon. All the germanium rectifiers were replaced with silicon during 1968-71. Diode power ratings were relatively low when they were first introduced for traction. In the original germanium rectifiers the load was shared between 1,280 diodes while in the silicon type there were 336 diodes.

The braking resistor was a vertical unit mounted inside the locomotive body above a cooling fan under the floor. The fan motor was connected across a section of the resistor and was driven by the voltage developed by the regenerated current. Originally the rheostatic brake was controlled by the power handle after operating a power/brake changeover switch, but the class was later modified to co-ordinate rheostatic braking with operation of the driver's automatic brake valve.

Alsthom suspension units and flexible drives were fitted as in Class 81.

Class 86 (AL6)

Number series: E3101-E3200†
Rated horsepower: 3,600hp
Equipment: Four AEI nose-suspended
Power supply: 25kVac overhead
Maximum speed: 100mph*

Wheel arrangement: Bo-Bo
Wheel diameter: 3ft 9.5in
Maximum TE: 58,000lb
Weight: 81ton 10cwt
First loco built: July 1965

Note: Above details refer to Class 86/0 and 86/3. 86/1 and 86/2 differ as follows:

* 86/0 now restricted to 80mph
† Later renumbered as 86.001-86.048, 86.101-86.103, 86.204-86.252. Members of 86/0 rebuilt as 86.253-86.261 and 86.311-86.329

Below:
General arrangement of 3,600hp Class 86/0 electric Bo-Bo.

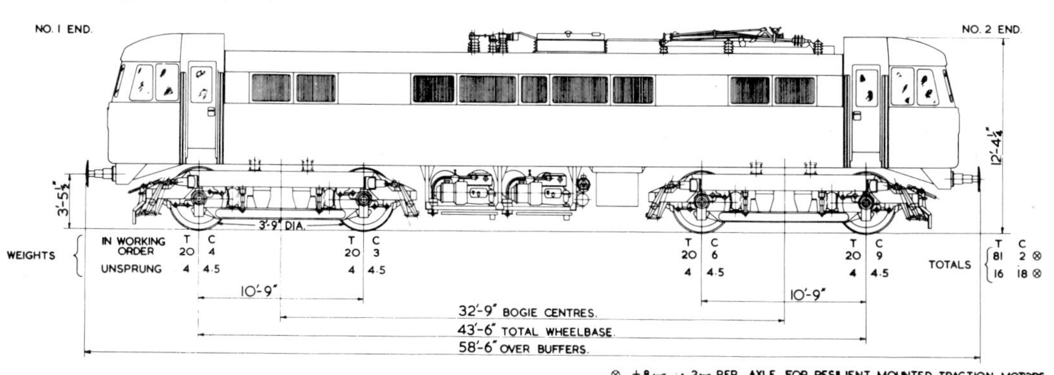

Class 86/1
Rated horsepower: 5,000hp
Weight: 85ton 8cwt

Class 86/2
Rated horsepower: 4,040hp
Weight: 83ton 13cwt

All members of 86/0 and 86/3 to be rebuilt from 1984 as Class 86/4, Nos 86.401-86.439.

With the LMR electrification between Liverpool, Manchester, Birmingham and Euston approaching completion, a further 100 Bo-Bo locomotives were ordered. These were all of the same design and designated Class 86. Electrical equipment was supplied by English Electric and AEI. Mechanical design was by BR, Doncaster, where 40 of the locomotives were built. The remaining 60 were built at English Electric's Vulcan Foundry works.

While similar in external appearance and specification to the preceding locomotives, Class 86 incorporated various changes based on experience with the prototypes. Each traction motor now had

Above:
Class 86/0, represented here by No 86.021 at Crewe on 27 August 1974, retains the original 'AL6' bogie design with axle-hung motors. The poor riding of locomotives so equipped led to them being down-graded to 80mph due to damage to the track and to bogie frames. *N. E. Preedy*

its own 'power pack' consisting of silicon rectifier, smoothing choke and blower connected to an individual secondary winding on a fixed-ratio transformer. The tap-changer was similar to the high-tension unit in Class 82 but modified in detail. Control gear for the traction motors was also divided into four groups and mounted on equipment frames adjacent to the respective power packs, the whole arrangement being dictated by the principle of easy isolation of a faulty power circuit and replacement of the equipment affected. The traction motors were designed to provide the required tractive effort/speed characteristic without field-weakening, with a consequent reduction in control gear.

The design change that had the most effect on the subsequent history of the class was rejection of flexible drives in favour of axle-hung suspension of the traction motors. Otherwise the original bogies were similar to Class 85. In Class 86 only one pantograph was fitted from the outset, and there was no provision for working on 6.25kV as this voltage was not used on the LMR electrification. Ten locomotives were equipped with the AEI 'crossed arm' pantograph later adopted throughout Class 87. Wheel diameter was 3ft 9in as compared with 4ft 0in in all the prototype classes.

After Class 86 had gone into service, complaints of bad riding and the increased incidence of broken rails led to numerous experiments with the suspension. The final result was the division of the class into Classes 86/0, 86/1, 86/2, 86/3 and 86/4 with the following characteristics (Classes 86/0 and 86/3 have multiple-unit control):

Class 86/0: Class 86 locomotives as built. Restricted as far as possible to services not requiring 100mph running and now down-graded to 80mph.

Class 86/1: Three locomotives equipped with bogies similar to those to be used in the future Class 87, having flexicoil suspension and frame-mounted motors with flexible drives. In the flexicoil system the body weight is carried by groups of coil springs, supported by platforms outside the bogie frames, which allow for lateral and rotational movements of the bogie as well as vertical springing.

Class 86/2: Locomotives with flexicoil suspension and SAB resilient wheels. The motors are axle-hung as before but half their weight is taken by rubber blocks in the construction of the wheel, greatly reducing shocks and stresses on the track and motors. The original type of motor, which could not be adapted to take a flexible drive, was retained. Converted locomotives were given new motors, although of the same type as before, and the gear ratio was raised.

Class 86/3: Class 86/0 locomotives fitted with SAB resilient wheels became Class 86/3. The modification reduced punishment of the track but the ride was still rough and the 86/3 is an 80mph locomotive although it can be used on 100mph services when necessary.

Class 86/4: Electrification in the Eastern Region to Norwich and Harwich brought a requirement for locomotives to work both 100mph Inter-City services and heavy express freight traffic. It was met by equipping Class 86/0 and 86/3 locomotives with flexicoil suspension, the 86/0s being given resilient wheels at the same time. Suspension and wheels were therefore similar to Class 86/2 but the gear ratio was unchanged. The locomotives treated in this way became Class 86/4.

After experiments with flexicoil secondary suspension and resilient wheels to reduce forces on the track, both were used in converting Class 86 locomotives to Class 86/2. The flexicoil springs are prominent in this view of 86.212 *Preston Guild* (named in April 1979) seen at Crewe on 1 September 1979. *K. Connolly*

Class 87

Number series: 87.001-87.035, 87.101
Rated horsepower: 5,000hp
Equipment: Four GEC fully suspended traction motors
Power supply: 25kVac overhead
Maximum speed: 110mph
Wheel arrangement: Bo-Bo
Wheel dia: 3ft 9.25in
Maximum TE: 58,000lb
Weight: 81ton 19cwt
First loco built: June 1973

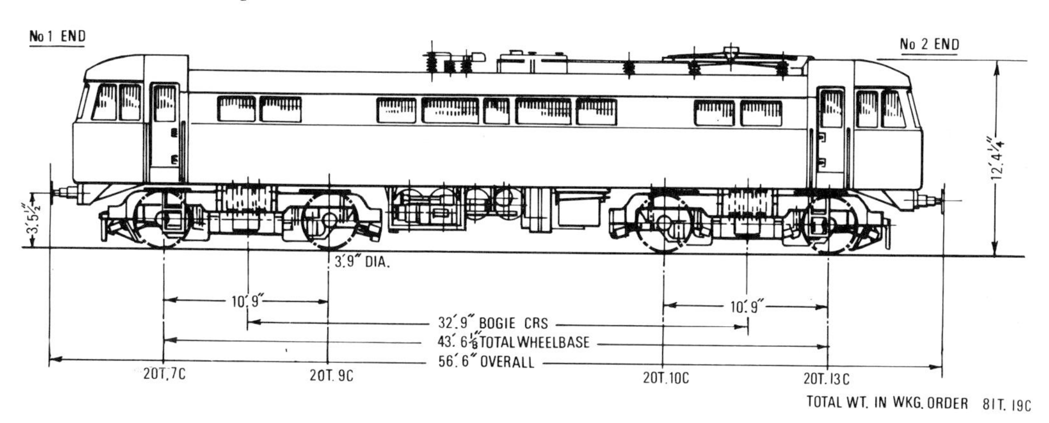

General arrangement of 5,000hp Class 87 electric Bo-Bo.

On the extension of 25kV ac electrification from Weaver Junction to Glasgow in 1974 the LMR supplemented its locomotive fleet with 35 locomotives of Class 87. These were the first 5,000hp locomotives on BR. The division of the electrical equipment into individual power packs, as in Class 86, was continued, but by now axle-hung motors at high speeds were suspect and the Class 87 motors were fully springborne in the bogie frames. They incorporated a new design of flexible drive in which the drive shaft passes through the hollow armature, to which it is coupled at one end by a gear type coupling. The other end of the shaft has a resilient rubber coupling to the pinion, which runs in separate bearings in an axle-hung gearcase. Field-weakening was not used in Class 86, but in Class 87 there is one weak-field step and the motors have compensating windings to improve commutation in weak-field conditions.

Control is by a high-tension tap-changer similar to the one in Classes 82 and 86 but with minor changes to improve reliability. The transformer is electrically identical to Class 86 but has a 20% higher rating because of the increased horsepower;

Above:
The final locomotive of the original 36 Class 87s built for the Glasgow electrification was selected for trials with thyristor control equipment. Although built in 1974, No 87.101 *Stephenson* was used for trials and did not enter capital stock until January 1979. A few weeks later it is seen heading the down 'Royal Scot' at Greenholm on 23 March 1979.
D. E. Canning

the capacity of the train-heating winding has also been raised to accommodate the higher demands of air-conditioned stock. Rheostatic braking is similar to Class 86. Locomotives of Class 87 were the first on BR to be equipped for working air-braked stock only. In addition to the control for the automatic air brake there is a separate lever for applying the straight air brake on the locomotive. The locomotives are fitted with sanding gear as well as incorporating the BR electronic system for controlling wheelspin. There is provision for working two locomotives in multiple.

Secondary suspension is by flexicoil springs as in Class 86 and there is a similar pivoting arrangement with rubber buffers controlling rotation of the bogie, but modification of the assembly has made the operation of lowering a locomotive on to its bogies easier. Class 87 locomotives were the first to be built with a headlight, which is placed centrally on the body ends just above the buffer beam.

A thirty-sixth locomotive was built to a similar specification but equipped with a thyristor control system. Carrying the number 87.101, it is at the time of writing (1984) the sole member of the 87.101 sub-class. Each of the four motor armatures is fed by two thyristor/diode bridges in series, and the field circuits are separately excited by similar circuits but with one bridge for each field. From zero to half armature voltage, the firing of the thyristors in one bridge is advanced while those in the bridge in series with it are cut off, the diodes in that bridge simply providing a path for the rectified current. When the thyristors in the first bridge are fully advanced, those in the second bridge come into action and supply a gradually increasing voltage in series with the voltage from the first bridge. When both bridges are fully advanced the motors receive their full operating voltage: the firing of the thyristors in the field circuits is then retarded to weaken the fields and allow acceleration to continue to full speed. Rheostatic braking effort is also controlled by the field circuit thyristors.

The locomotive can be controlled manually in the same way as Class 87/0 or the earlier ac locomotives but there is also provision for an 'advanced' driving mode. This enables the driver to preset tractive effort and speed. The locomotive will then accelerate to the selected speed at constant tractive effort; or if the motors are at full voltage before the speed is reached, acceleration will continue to the required level following the normal falling tractive effort characteristic.

Class 87 was originally designed for a maximum speed of 100mph in common with the other ac electric classes but in 1984 a start was made in fitting the class with BR/Brecknell-Willis pantographs, replacing the original 'crossed-arm' model, enabling the maximum speed to be raised to 110mph.

Class 87/2: In 1984/85 approval was given for the construction of 60 locomotives of Class 87/2, a development of '87/1', to be equipped with thyristor control. 25 locomotives are intended to replace the survivors of Classes 81, 82, 83 and 85 on the WCML, with 31 primarily for the ECML electrification and four to cover north London requirements.

Class 89

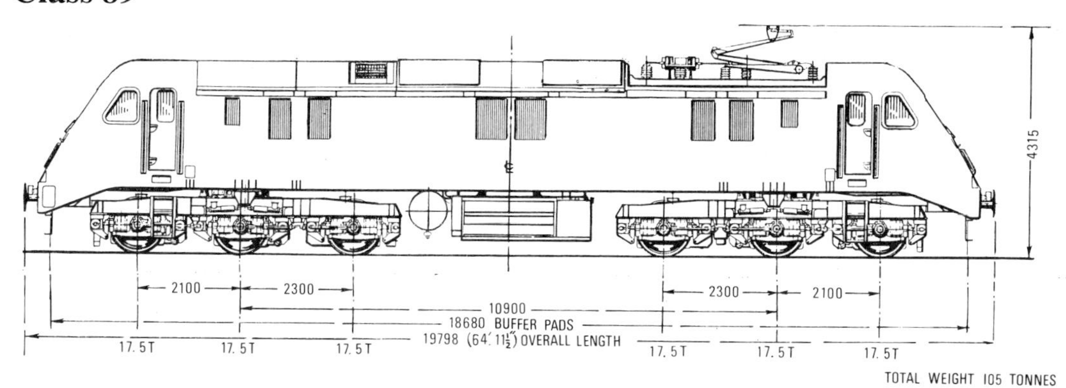

Above:
General arrangement of Class 89 electric Co-Co.

Proposals for a Co-Co locomotive for passenger and freight work on the ECML reached the prototype stage when Brush Electrical Machines Ltd was commissioned to supply the traction equipment for one locomotive to be built by BREL. This was due to begin trial running in 1985. A class of 33 locomotives, designated Class 89, was in view, coming into service as work on the East Coast electrification proceeds. The prototype has thyristor control and is designed for 125mph.

With the developing proposals for a Class 91 design for the ECML, by 1985 the requirement for the Class 89 was looking increasingly doubtful.

Below:
The prototype Class 89 locomotive under construction at Crewe works BREL in February 1985, seen resting on accommodation bogies.

8 Experimental Locomotives

In addition to the classes previously listed, there have also operated on British Railways several 'one off' locomotives which were not part of the regular motive power fleet. This includes such locomotives as Bulleid's 'Leader' which never operated service trains and *Kestrel* which did haul regular services but remained an experimental locomotive, and not part of the BR Fleet.

This chapter describes the most important of these locomotives but does not include the various experimental and departmental diesel shunter classes.

The 'Leader'

Number series: 36001-36005
Cylinders: Six, 12.25in × 15in
Heating surface: Tubes: 2,127sq ft
Firebox: 260sq ft
Superheater: 454sq ft
Total: 2,841sq ft
Grate area: 25.5sq ft*
Boiler pressure: 280lb/sq in

Wheel arrangement: 0-6-6-0T
Valve gear: Modified Bulleid
Driving wheel dia: 5ft 1in
TE at 85% pressure: 26,350lb
Weight: 130ton 10cwt
First loco built: June 1949
Loco withdrawn: November 1950

* Originally 43sq ft

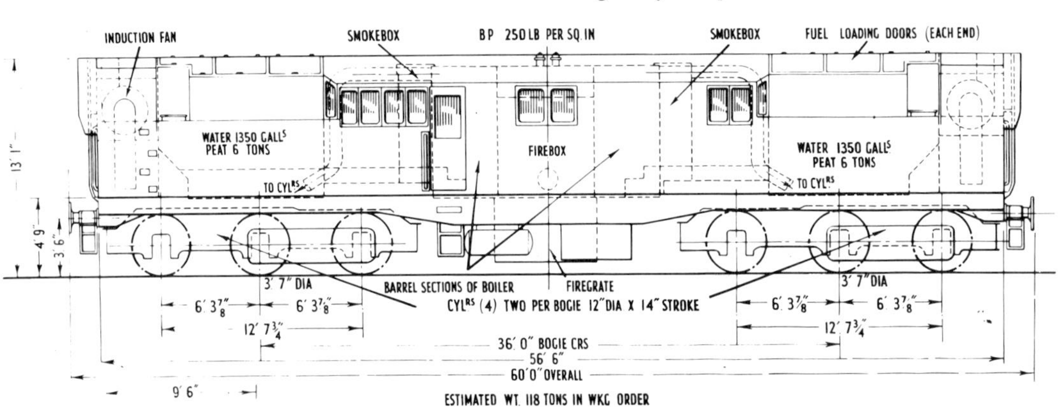

Above:
General arrangement of Bulleid 'Leader' class 0-6-6-0T.

Above right:
The highly unconventional 'Leader' class locomotive No 36001 is seen on trial with dynamometer car between Eastleigh and Guildford in August 1950. This locomotive never operated regular service trains. *S. C. Townroe*

In his 'Leader' locomotive of 1949 O. V. S. Bulleid set out to achieve a boiler without firebox legs and flat stayed surfaces, a radically new design of mixed-traffic steam locomotive. The result was an unusual layout with the fireman's position at the middle of the locomotive and a cab at each end. The locomotive was carried on two three-axle bogies, in each of which a three-cylinder steam engine drove the centre axle direct and the other two by chain drive. Steam distribution was by sleeve valves operated by a form of Walschaerts valve gear. Boiler and fuel supplies were enclosed by a

semi-streamlined casing. As designed, the fireman's compartment was likely to prove intolerably hot, and the off-centre position of the firegrate called for a different technique of firing. The chain drive gave trouble, particularly at starting, because stretch in the chains could disturb the even transmission of torque. There were numerous problems with the locomotive on test runs, in particular with poor steaming and crank-axle failures. Additionally the need to install ballast weights to balance the locomotive rendered it far too heavy. The first 'Leader', No 36001, made a number of trial runs on the Southern Region and construction of four more locomotives of the same design was put in hand. With Bulleid's retirement from British Railways, however, work on them was stopped and No 36001 was scrapped.

The prototype 'Deltic'

Engines: Two Napier 18-25 Deltic
Cylinders: Eighteen
Rating: 1,650hp at 1,500rpm
Transmission: Six EE axle-hung, nose-suspended traction motors
Maximum speed: 100mph
Wheel arrangement: Co-Co
Wheel dia: 3ft 7in
Maximum TE: 60,000lb
Weight: 106ton
Loco built: December 1955
Loco withdrawn: March 1961

Below:
General arrangement of English Electric 3,300hp diesel-electric Co-Co *Deltic*.

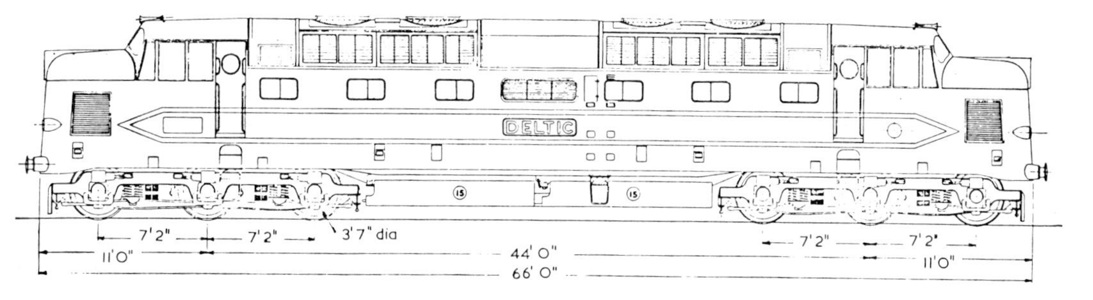

Above:
The prototype *Deltic* locomotive is seen at speed in its unique light blue livery. The success of this locomotive built by English Electric in 1955 led to the construction of the 22 members of Class 55 for the East Coast main line. In this view *Deltic* is hauling the 14.10 Liverpool-Euston near Rugby on 29 April 1958. *M. Mensing*

On its appearance in 1955 the 3,300hp prototype English Electric 'Deltic' locomotive was the most powerful single-unit diesel in the world. Its nearest rival was a Fairbanks-Morse diesel of 2,400hp in the USA. Both locomotives were of Co-Co wheel arrangement, but in spite of being powered by two engine-generator sets, the 'Deltic' weighed only 106ton against the 124ton of the US locomotive. The 'Deltic' design sprang from the conviction of Sir George (later Lord) Nelson of the English Electric Co Ltd that a diesel locomotive could be built which would hold its own in power/weight ratio and performance with the best contemporary electrics, particularly in France. The Napier company in the English Electric Group had developed a lightweight, high-speed, opposed-piston two stoke for fast naval patrol boats, naming it 'Deltic' from its triangular shape, the three banks of six cylinders forming an inverted triangle with a crankshaft at each corner. Nelson chose this engine for his locomotive experiment, running counter to the BR preference for relatively heavy medium-speed engines, which was resulting in A1A-A1A and 1Co-Co1 designs. The two engines in the prototype developed 1,650hp at 1,500rpm, being downrated from the 2,500hp of the naval engine to extend the time between maintenance in rail service conditions. On completion in 1955 the locomotive was finished in a blue livery with yellow lining and carried the name *Deltic* on the bodysides. From 1955 to 1959 it was given the opportunity to show its paces on the WCML, and in 1959 was transferred to the Eastern Region, where hopes of electrification to Edinburgh in the foreseeable future were low but the management had faith in the potential of high-speed services. *Deltic* worked on the ECML until 1961, restricted by clearance problems for the most part to journeys between King's Cross, Doncaster and Leeds. There were accordingly some dimensional changes in the 22 Class 55 'Deltic' locomotives ordered by the Eastern Region to implement its high-speed train policy. The original 'Deltic' was withdrawn after a failure in 1961. In 1963 it was presented to the Science Museum in London as representing a significant step forward in the evolution of diesel rail traction. The soundness of the mechanical design was underlined by the increase of its maximum speed during its time in service from the design figure of 95mph to 100mph, still with notable smoothness of riding. A commentator in 1962 remarked that 'extraordinary haulage and acceleration capacities relative to other English motive power were obtained' and went on to note that the still lighter (99ton) production locomotives were even enhancing the performance of the prototype.

DP2

Number: DP2
Engine: English Electric 16CSVT
Cylinders: Sixteen
Rating: 2,700hp at 850rpm
Transmission: Six EE axle-hung, nose-suspended traction motors
Maximum speed: 90mph
Wheel arrangement: Co-Co
Wheel dia: 3ft 6in
Maximum TE: 50,000lb
Weight: 105ton
Loco built: February 1962
Loco withdrawn: July 1967

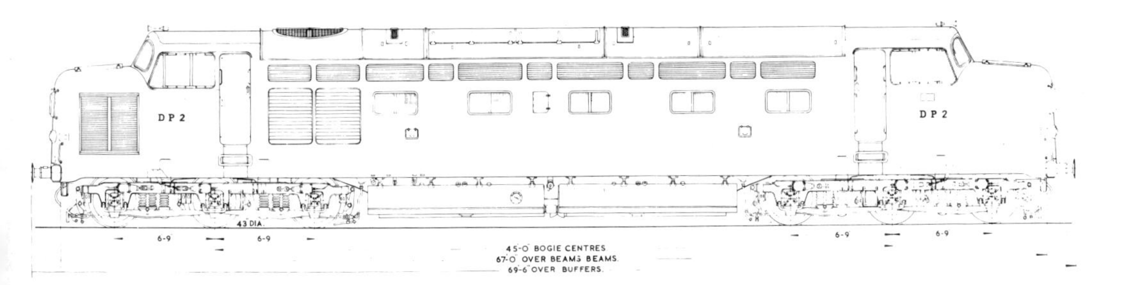

Above:
General arrangement of English Electric 2,700hp diesel-electric Co-Co No DP2. *R. S. Carter*

The English Electric DP2 locomotive was the company's response to a specification issued in 1960 by the British Transport Commission for diesel locomotives able to maintain average speeds of 75mph on inter-city journeys up to 300 miles. It was assumed at that time that the cream of passenger traffic over longer distances would go to internal airlines. The English Electric 16-cylinder vee engine originally fitted in Nos 10000/1 had been developed to give 2,000hp and was powering the company's D200 class. The addition of charge-air cooling raised the output to 2,700hp, and in this form the engine could be fitted into the same body as a production 'Deltic'. The 22 'Deltics' for the ECML were going through the shops at this time and the new locomotive closely followed their design apart from internal changes made necessary by having one large engine-generator set instead of two smaller ones of the characteristic 'Deltic' form. DP2 stood for 'Diesel Prototype 2', another 'Deltic'

Below:
Another successful English Electric prototype was DP2 of 1962. Although given a production Deltic style body and livery, it contained a conventional 2,700hp engine. The success of DP2 gave rise to the 50 members of Class 50 with the same power unit but DP2 itself was damaged beyond repair in an accident and cut up. It is seen here leaving King's Cross. *English Electric Co*

link in that the prototype 'Deltic' had been DP1. The bogies, too, were identical to those of the production 'Deltics' and Class 37s. DP2 had rivals in the *Lion* prototype from a BRCW/AEI/Sulzer consortium, and *Falcon* from Brush but it was some 10ton lighter than either. It was turned out from the Vulcan Foundry on 2 May 1962 and after some convincing demonstrations of its powers on test trains was soon in revenue service between Euston and Liverpool. After other duties on the WCML, DP2 was transferred to the Eastern Region in 1963 and took up standard 'Deltic' diagrams. Meanwhile BR had made an agreement with English Electric to lease 50 new locomotives with similar power plant and bogies but various 'sophistications'. These locomotives formed Class 50. DP2 continued a successful career until 31 July 1967, when while working the 12.00 King's Cross to Edinburgh its path was fouled by the derailed wagons of a freight train. Seven passengers were killed and 45 injured in the ensuing collision, unavoidable even with emergency braking from 80mph, and DP2 suffered severe damage. It was broken up in 1968, still with its builder's number.

Lion

Number: D0260
Engine: Sulzer 12LDA28-C
Cylinders: Twelve
Rating: 2,750hp at 800rpm
Transmission: Six AEI axle-hung, nose-suspended traction motors
Maximum speed: 100mph
Wheel arrangement: Co-Co
Wheel dia: 3ft 9in
Maximum TE: 55,000lb
Weight: 114ton
Loco built: April 1962
Loco withdrawn: October 1963

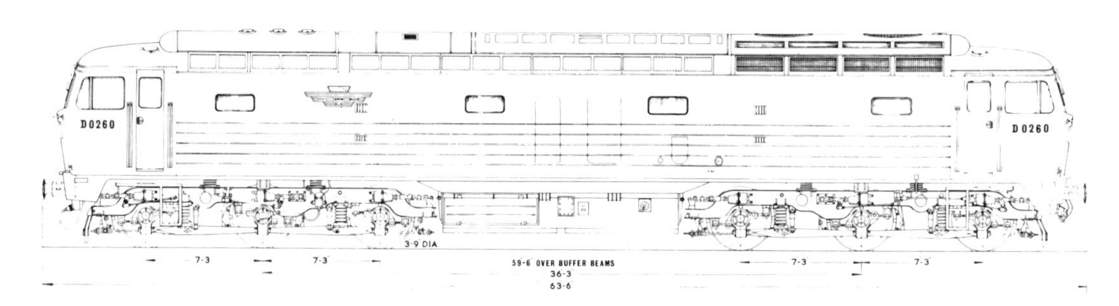

Above:
General arrangement of BRCW 2,750hp diesel-electric Co-Co *Lion*. *R. S. Carter*

Below:
The BRCW/Sulzer prototype locomotive No D0260 *Lion* contained the power unit which would be fitted to the ubiquitous Class 47. *Lion* is seen in its unique and distinctive white livery passing Beeston Junction.

In an attempt to capture an order for a class of type 4 locomotives of more advanced design and better power/weight ratio than the cumbersome English Electric D200 class and the 'Peaks', in 1962 the Birmingham Railway Carriage & Wagon Company in association with Sulzer and AEI built D0260 *Lion*. Its engine was a development of that fitted to the 'Peaks' and AEI electrical equipment was fitted. *Lion* was built in competition with D0280 *Falcon* (see Class 53), built by Brush and powered by two high speed Maybach engines with Brush traction motors.

At this time, however, BRCW were in serious financial difficulties and not in a position to undertake construction of the new type 4 class. However, although *Falcon* was a successful locomotive, high speed diesel engines were not universally popular at British Railways. The final decision was for a locomotive similar in appearance to *Lion* and equipped with the Sulzer engine, but built by Brush with their own traction equipment. This was the standard Brush type 4, later Class 47 (q.v.).

GT3

Number: GT3
Engine: Gas turbine of 9,000rpm
Rating: 2,750hp
Transmission: Mechanical gearbox and flexible drive
Maximum speed: 90mph
Wheel dia: 5ft 9in
Wheel arrangement: 4-6-0
Driving wheel dia: 4ft 0.5in
Maximum TE: 60,000lb
Weight: Loco: 79ton 16cwt
Tender: 44ton
Loco built: May 1961
Loco withdrawn: December 1962

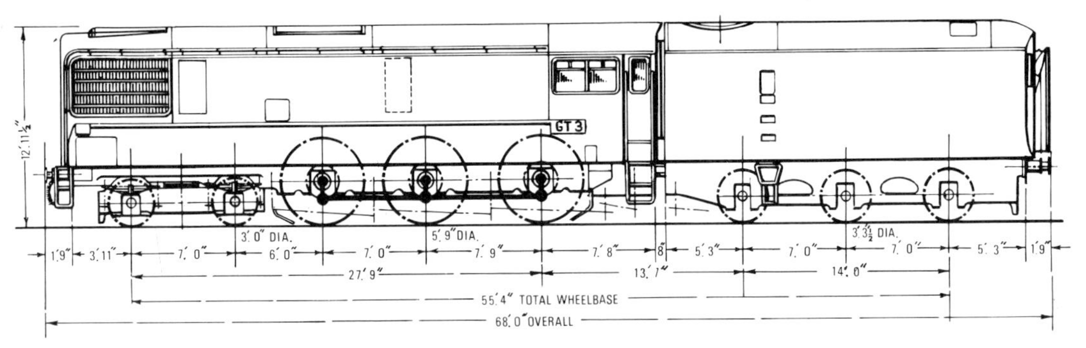

Above:
General arrangement of English Electric gas turbine 4-6-0 No GT3.

Below:
One prototype design which led to nothing was the Vulcan Foundry-built gas turbine locomotive GT3, seen here at Marylebone goods yard. The steam locomotive style chassis and tender are clearly visible.

By the 1960s developments in gas turbine technology encouraged the English Electric Co Ltd to build a prototype locomotive powered in this way. A mechanical transmission based on industrial practice was used, the power turbine being coupled to a gearbox on the centre axle of a fixed wheelbase chassis, with coupling rods to the other two axles. A leading four-wheel bogie and the six coupled wheels followed conventional practice for a 4-6-0 steam locomotive, while the 'bonnet' enclosure of the machinery on the main frames was not unlike a streamlined boiler casing. A separate tender carrying fuel supplies and a train-heating boiler increased the similarity to a steam locomotive. Problems with the coupling between power turbine and gearbox delayed the trials 'on the road' but in 1961 the locomotive emerged from the Vulcan Foundry for experimental running on various sections of the LMR. In practice, however, the improvements in gas turbines since the Brown-Boveri and Metropolitan-Vickers locomotives proved insufficient to challenge diesel and electric power and the experiment lapsed, although GT3 was by no means unsuccessful in its performance on the road. Gas turbines were used again on BR in the prototype APT, but with electric transmission. This train has found a resting place in the National Railway Museum, English Electric's gas turbine locomotive, GT3, is no more.

E1000/E2001

See No 18100 p40

Number: E2001†
Rated horsepower: 2,500hp
Equipment: Four MV nose-suspended traction motors
Power supply: 25kVac overhead
Maximum speed: 90mph

Wheel arrangement: AIA-AIA
Wheel dia: 3ft 8in
Maximum TE: 40,000lb
Weight: 109ton
Loco built: 1958*
Loco withdrawn: April 1968

* Rebuilt from gas turbine locomotive 18100 built 1951
† Formerly 18100. Initially renumbered E1000

Below:
In order to provide driver training facilities for the London Midland ac electrification, the former gas turbine locomotive 18100 was rebuilt by Metropolitan-Vickers as an A1A-A1A 25kV electric locomotive. At first it was numbered E1000 but this was soon altered to E2001. Seen at East Didsbury temporary depot in August 1959, soon after conversion, the locomotive never entered regular service. *T. K. Widd*

Conversion of the Western Region gas turbine locomotive No 18100 into an ac electric locomotive for driver training on the LMR has been mentioned briefly earlier. The work began in January 1958 at the Stockton-on-Tees works of Metropolitan-Vickers. On its completion the locomotive emerged in the late autumn as No E1000 and began driver training runs on the Manchester-Wilmslow via Styal line. No E1000 was now an A1A-A1A of 2,500hp the motors driving the middle axle of each bogie having been removed. Weight was 105ton as against the 130ton of the gas turbine Co-Co. In October 1959 the locomotive was renumbered E2001. This was BR's first ac locomotive. In most respects the electrical equipment was similar to the Bo-Bo prototypes which were still under construction but the mercury-arc rectifiers were glass bulbs of a type widely used in traction substations. Like the steel tank rectifiers which had been developed from industrial designs for the prototype locomotives, they did not need pumps for maintaining the vacuum. The choice of a rectifier primarily intended for stationary duties was dictated by availability and the fact that E2001 was a stopgap until the first 'AL1' (now Class 81) locomotives were delivered. During its brief career the locomotive worked also in the Liverpool and Crewe areas, and on the Glasgow suburban lines north of the Clyde for electrification tests. By 1960 some 1,300 drivers had been trained and the first AL1s and AL2s were coming into service. To reduce the number of trains operated for training, a simulator was installed at Willesden and part of the programme carried out with its aid. Periods of storage followed for E2001 and after withdrawal in 1968 it was sold for scrap in 1972.

Kestrel

Number: HS4000
Engine: Sulzer 16LVA24
Cylinders: Sixteen
Rating: 4,000hp at 1,100rpm
Transmission: Six Brush nose-suspended traction motors
Wheel arrangement: Co-Co
Wheel dia: 3ft 9in
Maximum TE: 70,000lb
Weight: 126ton
Loco built: January 1968
Loco withdrawn: January 1971

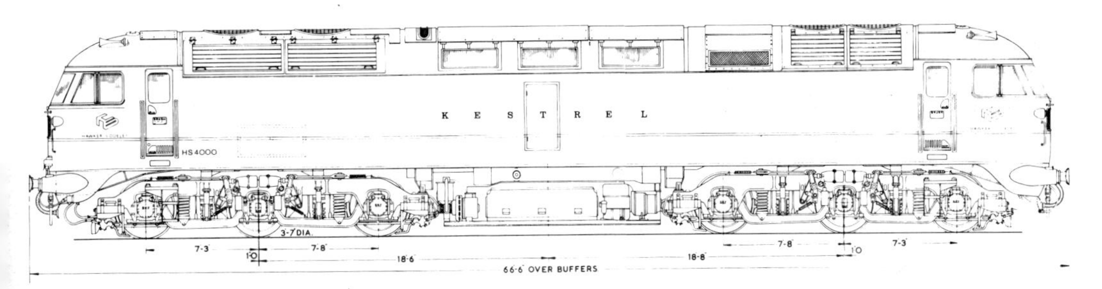

Above:
General arrangement of Brush (Hawker-Siddeley) 4,000hp diesel-electric No HS4000 *Kestrel*. *R. S. Carter*

The Brush/Sulzer combination was responsible for the first single-engined 4,000hp diesel locomotive in the world. On 28 January the Brush Electrical Engineering Co Ltd handed over to British Railways for trial running a 4,000hp prototype which carried the name *Kestrel* in line with the naming tradition of the company's Falcon works at Loughborough. The diesel engine was the Sulzer 16LVA24, a 16-cylinder version of the 12LDA28 which powers the Class 47 locomotives. New ground was broken in the use of brushless alternators as main and auxiliary generators, and in an extended use of electronics in the control system, based on experience already gained. A small number of standard plug-in printed circuit cards were used in various combinations to provide a variety of control functions. The lightweight semi-streamlined body of the locomotive was carried on two three-axle bogies with one-piece cast steel Commonwealth type frames. Primary and secondary suspensions were conventional, with coil springs in both stages and axleboxes moving vertically between parallel guides. Weight in working order was 133ton (design weight 126ton). Although designed for 125mph, *Kestrel* was restricted in its performance on BR by its axleload. The maximum allowed for locomotives with axle-hung motors was 100mph, axleload not to exceed 20ton. In 1969 *Kestrel* was equipped with Class 47 bogies, but its continuous rating was lowered by the smaller motors. Weight was reduced, however, and the locomotive took up passenger workings between King's Cross and Newcastle in October 1969 after further tests on the ECML. These duties were short-lived and Kestrel returned to freight work. While BR engineers remained cool to the idea of a high-power general-purpose locomotive, turning to the HST concept for fast passenger work, *Kestrel* attracted the interest of the Soviet Railways, who asked Brush if they would exhibit it at a railway exhibition at Shcherbinka in 1971. After negotiations, however, the USSR agreed to buy the locomotive and ship it to Russia, where it would be exhibited and then turned over to other uses. *Kestrel* accordingly left its homeland for ever in April 1971. The locomotive was never numbered by BR but carried its own number, HS4000.

Below:
The very advanced Brush/Hawker Siddeley prototype No HS4000 *Kestrel* seen at King's Cross whilst operating on East Coast main line express services. The first 4,000hp diesel to operate on BR, it did not however gain any orders and was eventually sold to the Soviet Union.

Appendices

1 Diesel locomotive control systems

Diesel engine speed is controlled by a governor. In some of the early BR diesel classes a limited number of governor settings could be selected by the driver, chosen so that the corresponding speeds were clear of certain critical values at which torsional vibrations might damage the crankshaft. Later design shifted the critical speeds outside the operating range and so speed could be continuously variable between idling and maximum.

In locomotives with 'stepped' (as distinct from continuous) speed control, the governor is set for the desired speed by pistons acting on a lever system. The pistons are operated by oil or air under pressure, which is admitted to the speed control cylinders by energising electromagnetic valves in various combinations. When continuous speed control became practicable it was effected by the direct action on the governor of compressed air fed through a self-lapping valve in the driver's controller. Many locomotives with this form of control can work in multiple with those of other classes similarly equipped, but certain differences in detail on control systems may prevent this. Engine speed control is only one of the functions to be provided in multiple working, and electrical as well as pneumatic interconnections are necessary. Locomotives of Classes 50, 56 and 58, for example can only work in multiple with others of the same class.

Some locomotive classes which work MGR trains are equipped with a slow speed control for travel at 'crawling' speed through loading and unloading plants. The engine is set to run at idling or other predetermined speed and an electronic control takes over, based on signals from a speedometer reading between 0 and 3mph. The signals control the frequency of a chopper in the main generator field circuit. In locomotives of Classes 20, 33, 47 and 50 equipped with this control, the driver sets the speed to be maintained with a potentiometer, adjusting it as necessary during the slow-speed operation. In Classes 56 and 58, three speeds are selected with a switch and are held accurately without the driver's intervention.

When Class 27 locomotives worked the Edinburgh-Glasgow high-speed service push-pull, with one locomotive at each end of the train, both were interconnected by the engine speed control air line. With longer formations there would be an unacceptable lag in the response of the locomotive under remote control and so in the HSTs electromagnetic control of an oil servo system is adopted. An electro-pneumatic system is used for remote control of Class 47 locomotives working Glasgow-Edinburgh push-pull services, with the special feature that only two wires are needed to convey the control signals. Both systems adjust the engine speed in steps, but with trains such as these which vary little in weight, continuously variable control is unnecessary.

2 Dual braking

In the early stages of diesel and electric traction development on BR, the vacuum brake was the standard equipment for vehicles. Locomotives were fitted with a straight air brake, ie a brake applied by the direct admission of air from a reservoir to the brake cylinders. When working vacuum-braked trains, the driver's vacuum valve controlled the train brakes and also made a proportional application of the locomotive brakes. A separate air brake valve was provided for applying the locomotive brakes when running light.

The later adoption of the air brake made it necessary for locomotives to be able to control brakes of both types. This is the meaning of the term 'dual braked'. It does not mean that there are two types of brake on the locomotive, which still has air brakes only.

When a dual braked locomotive is hauling air braked stock, the driver's air brake valve controls the brakes on the train and on the locomotive. In this case the locomotive brake no longer operates as a straight air brake but is controlled, like the train brakes, by dropping the pressure in the brake pipe running through the train. It is therefore an automatic brake because a fault or break in the pipe applies the brakes, the fall in pressure operating valves which connect the air reservoirs to the brake cylinders.

If the locomotive is hauling vacuum braked stock, the exhausters are switched on and this automatically brings an air/vacuum relay valve into operation. Movement of the air brake valve in the cab then applies the vacuum brakes on the train and the air brakes on the locomotive, the latter again being applied by a reduction of air pressure. There is also an independent control for operating the locomotive brakes as straight air brakes when running light.

Left:
The control desk of a Class 87 Bo-Bo 25kV electric locomotive, introduced 1973. *BR*

Below:
Class 87 locomotive No 87.012 *Coeur de Lion* in the latest British Rail Intercity livery.